THE PROVENCE BOOK

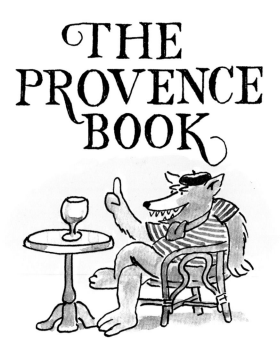

A Guide, with Fables

HUNTLEY BALDWIN

WHITE WILLOW PUBLISHING

White Willow Publishing
Box 6464
Jackson, Wyoming 83002

EAN/ISBN-13 978-0-9755359-7-4
PRINTING 1 2 3 4 5 6 7 8 9 10

Printed in China

To Joan. A loaf of bread, a jug of wine and thou,
plus a house in Provence.

Introduction

Americans, here are some things you should know about Provence: There are no Starbucks where you can grab a coffee to go. Stores close capriciously and everything except restaurants shuts down between noon and two p.m. People drive like maniacs to get to a shop where they will stand and chat endlessly with the clerk. Rosé wine is socially acceptable. Lunch in a restaurant can last two hours or more. There are no such things as "early bird specials" or "doggie bags." Cars park on the sidewalks. The loaf of bread you buy fresh in the morning is "stale" by dinnertime. And, most annoyingly, everybody speaks in French.

You aren't in Kansas anymore. Daily life here is different than it is at home. You could easily spend half your day shopping for food and the rest of the day preparing and eating it. A cup of coffee that you could easily down in two gulps can stretch into an hour's entertainment. For the tourist accustomed to tight schedules and structured days, the relaxed pace of life in Provence takes some getting used to.

Our advice is to choose a central location (ideally in or near a small town with services), rent a house for as long as you can, rent a car and then settle in and pretend you live there. Even if your time is limited and you are staying in hotels, don't try to do or see too much. In the words of the sports cliché, let the game come to you. Sip coffee at a sidewalk cafe. Mosey through the countryside. Have a picnic lunch. Taste wine at a vineyard. Walk the narrow streets of a "village perché." Poke into shops and galleries. Wander through an outdoor market. And, if you must, visit an historic site or museum.

A friend who was asked what he liked best about his trip to Provence replied, "Being there." He got it. Calvin Trillin describes this low-key approach to travel as "hanging around." As much as anything Provence is a frame of mind.

That's why this book is as much about how to get along in Provence as what to see in Provence (although we do have a lot of suggestions for this, too.) Joan and I have rented five different houses there on twelve occasions. During that time we've made our share of discoveries and suffered our share of embarrassments and frustrations (you'll see these reflected in the "fables.")

We've found that the best coping mechanism is a sense of humor. As one visitor said of the drivers in Provence, "they amuse me." It is our hope that what follows will amuse as well as inform you.

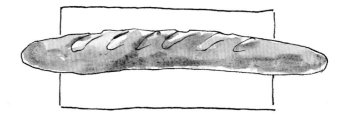

PROVENCE
Côtes-du-Rhône
VAISON-la-ROMAINE
Séguret
DENTELLES
Mt VENTOUX
RHÔNE
ORANGE
Gigondas
Chateauneuf-du-Pape
Beaumes-de-Venise
Tavel
Côtes-du-Ventoux
Sault
Pont-du-Gard
AVIGNON
Gordes
Rousillon
GARD
L'Isle-sur-la-Sorgue
Apt
Côtes-du-Luberon
Tarascon
Beaucaire
St Rémy
Bonnieux
LUBERONS
Les Baux
ALPILLES
Lourmarin
NÎMES
DURANCE
VERDON
Côtes-des-Baux
ARLES
Coteaux-d'Aix-en-Provence
CAMARGUE
Mt Ste VICTOIRE
AIX-en-PROVENCE
Aigues-Mortes
ETANG DE BERRE
Marignane Airport
Côtes-de-Provence
SPAIN
MARSEILLE
NICE
N
le Castellet
Bandol
Cassis
La Ciotat
Bandol
TOULON
MEDITERRANEAN
PARIS
FRANCE

The Bell-Ringer of Puyvert

Long ago, at the base of the Luberon mountains, lay the sleepy village of Puyvert. It had no cafes, no church, no boulangerie. It was so quiet in Puyvert that all the residents had to do was sleep. They slept so often they lost all track of time. Finally the villagers held a meeting to discuss their problem. "I know what to do!" It was the village idiot and he had a plan. The villagers listened and they agreed: "It's idiotic, but it just might work." They built an iron cage atop the village hall and hung a bell in it. The idiot's job was to ring the bell every hour, one chime for one o'clock, two chimes for two o'clock, etc. Everyone would now know the time, day or night. Weeks later, as he had every night, a villager awakened to the sound of twelve chimes. Two minutes later, after he'd fallen back to sleep, the bell rang twelve times again. "Someday," he muttered sleepily, "We'll have to get rid of that idiot." But they never did.

moral:

Sometimes it's hard to sleep in even the sleepiest village.

Silent nights

Our first night in Provence was an eye-opener. We had rented a house in the village of Puyvert in the Luberon. The house was tucked under the bell tower of the *mairie* (village hall) and next to a parking lot. It was a charming Provençal iron bell tower that allows strong winds to blow through. But it lost its charm when we were awakened every hour on the hour and again on the half hour by a bell seemingly inches from our bedroom. The 12 chimes that marked midnight were especially trying.

You'll also want to avoid parking lots when selecting a house or hotel room. Teens on motorbikes roared in and out of the lot outside our window. There were car engines starting and revving and car doors slamming at all hours.. The municipal trash truck with its annoying back-up beeper arrived at dawn to manhandle the dumpsters.

Not even a house in the country can guarantee a peaceful night's sleep. One house we rented was next door to a swimming pool where local frogs gathered for late-night parties. Then there were the dogs. One or more dogs prowled behind the fences, walls and hedges of every Provençal *mas* and served as another layer of protection for privacy minded owners. Some particularly noisy dogs lived and barked at the farm near our house. When we mentioned them to our landlady she said, yes, she knew of these dogs. In fact, she had once called the owner about the barking and had been told in no uncertain French that if she didn't like it she should move to the city. We decided, wisely I think, not to approach the owner with our complaints.

Then there was the wind chime that hung over the terrace beneath our open bedroom window. My personal rule would be that people who live in the vicinity of *mistrals* (the infamous insanity-producing north winds of Provence that often blow for days at a time) shouldn't hang out tinkling wind chimes. Even a gentle breeze made it sound like a Good Humor truck was parked next to our bedroom all night. However, on those nights when the mistral did blow the wind noise easily drowned out the tinkle of the chimes.

Mistral

A typical mas is built facing southwest to minimize the impact of the mistral. It usually has no windows on the north side.
The gentle slope of the roof is to help prevent tiles from blowing off.

The incredible flying tart

One there was a woman who didn't believe everything she read. She had read about the famous wind of Provence called the *mistral* that blows down the Rhône valley from the north and according to one book, "…knocks off roof tiles and sets doors banging, getting on everyone's nerves." The woman, who came from a country that had hurricanes, was unimpressed by the prospect of such a wind. Such a wind was beginning to blow on the day she stopped by the patisserie to buy a strawberry tart. The clerk put the tart into a flimsy cardboad box and tied it with a ribbon. When the woman stepped outside, a gust of wind lifted the box from her hand. As she watched in disbelief the tart flew a short distance before smashing into a gooey mess on the sidewalk.

moral:

Yes, Virginia, there *is* a mistral.

A walk to Lourmarin

For many years each May we rented a house in the tiny village of Puyvert. A favorite activity (indeed, about the only activity in Puyvert) was to walk to Lourmarin, a larger nearby Town.

On this day as we set out some men are playing **boules** in the parking lot behind the Mairie (town hall). The bell in the tower rings out the hour, as it did all night long. We pass the atelier of a couple who make **santons**, the traditional crèche figures of Provence. He sculpts the clay figures and she makes the costumes from Provençal fabrics. In the tiny **place** (square) two old women sit on a stone bench near an old **lavoir**, in the shade of a graceful plane tree.

The road from the place climbs gently toward the Luberons and we pass some restored maisons secondaires reflecting the renewed interest in the region as an escape from city life, and a small messy farm that has stubbornly resisted gentrification.

As we turn toward Lourmarin its château is visible above the trees. Our road passes a field of green wheat dotted with bright red poppies. On the other side, white, yellow and purple wildflowers are sprinkled through the field in front of a stone farm house (mas). On closer examination the ground cover reveals aromatic herbs -- rosemary and thyme. Another turn of the road yields the promise of tastes to come: olive, almond and cherry trees.

Behind them are vineyards showing the early signs of grapes that will become Côtes du Luberon wines.

Just before reaching town we come upon the Château du Lourmarin, part 15th Century, part Renaissance, standing behind a grove of olive trees. To the right is the often-photographed low skyline of Lourmarin.

Today is market day, so the tree-lined street that borders the soccer field is crowded with the vans and stalls of the sellers of baskets, fabrics, fresh fruits and vegetables and much more. We buy a loaf of bread and a slab of "mountain cheese" for lunch and some white asparagus for dinner, reluctantly passing up a stall where chickens turn tantalizingly on spits.

After the market we look into the local wine cooperative where you can buy **vin du pays** by the bottle or pumped from large vats into plastic jugs. Continuing into town we check out the menus posted in front of several restaurants, stop at the **tabac** for a Herald Tribune and finally settle in at a table in front of the café next door for coffees.

In the course of our 30-minute walk we have encapsulated the essence of what makes Provence Provence: boules and bell towers; santons and sunshine; flowers and herbs; farm houses and châteaux; orchards and vineyards; wines and restaurants; open-air markets and outdoor cafés. All to be savored at the leisurely pace of a stroll in the country.

Which is the very pace at which we encourage you to experience Provence.

The Lure of Lourmarin

Lourmarin makes an ideal home base for touring the Luberons and beyond. It has all the necessities: three cafés, three boulangeries, a tabac (source of Herald Tribunes), wine cooperative, tiny grocery store, post office, bank and gas station. There are plenty of good restaurants, including two, Le Moulin de Lourmarin and Auberge la Fenière, that have earned Michelin stars. It's a 30-minute drive from Aix-en-Provence if you need a city. And it sits at the base of the *Comb de Lourmarin*, a hair-raising road that winds up through the Luberons to Bonnieux and other popular hill towns. Tourists are attracted by its château, which sits across a meadow from town, the many trendy shops and galleries, a cemetery in which Albert Camus is buried and one of the prettiest "skylines" you'll see in Provence.

Part 15th century, part Renaissance, the château is open for tours daily except Tuesdays. English-speaking tours can be arranged.

Le Château

To Bonnieux via Combe de Lourmarin

Back road to Puyvert

D943

Wine Coop. Fill'er up with Côtes du Luberon

W.C.

Friday market up here, too

Friday market held along here

Soccer field

Playground

W.C.

Le Château

Moulin de Lourmarin

Where the action is. Café de L'Ormeau and Café Gaby plus Tabac, shops and art galleries.

Walk to Puyvert

L'Eglise

Silo house (private)

Residential Lourmarin Several streets wind up to it from main drag

Skyline view photo op

One-way. Main auto "cruising" route through town

D27

Albert Camus sleeps here →

To Puyvert and Lauris

Sitting at "our" café

The first time we arrived in Puyvert to take possession of our rental house we got there early and had time to kill. We drove to the nearby town of Lourmarin, found a table at Café de L'Ormeau and ordered a glass of wine. We soon realized two things: if you're visiting Provence, Lourmarin is a terrific town to be near. And Café de L'Ormeau is a terrific place to kill time.

L'Ormeau is one of three cafés in the heart of town. It sits on a tiny "square" next to a tabac and across the street from Café Gaby. (Café La Fontaine is just around the corner yet somehow feels removed from the action.) The cobblestone street that separates Gaby and L'Ormeau is one-way for cars but is mostly used for pedestrian strolling. Except to make a delivery or pick up cigarettes at the tabac, there is no reason to drive through town on this road. You make the drive only to see or be seen.

The two cafés share an "annex"--tables under umbrellas on a patch of sidewalk across the street--and waiters shuttle back and forth, deftly avoiding cars. We were seated in L'Ormeau's section of the annex when a local dog decided to do its business in the middle of the street. A waiter from Gaby saw it about to happen and ran out to shoo away the dog. He was too late. He looked down at the pile and may have briefly considered cleaning it up. Instead, he made a mental note of the location and simply avoided it on his trips back and forth. We settled back to see who would not be so lucky. A woman wearing open-toed sandals missed it by inches. A passing car flattened a corner of it. A few more misses, then a boy on a motorbike hit it squarely. Finally, a young father pushing a stroller over the rough stones took home what remained on the bottom of his shoe. It was like watching a Jacques Tati movie.

L'Ormeau epitomizes the pleasures of café sitting. For the price of a glass of wine you can enjoy the passing parade. Once you find a table it's yours for as long as you wish. No waiter will pressure you to pay up and move on. In fact, a few times we've had to go inside to find our waiter and settle up.

The Wolf who cried Boy

There once was a wolf who liked nothing more than sitting at a sidewalk cafe. On sunny afternoons you'd find him nursing a beer and watching the world go by. On just such an afternoon he seated himself at a cafe to order a beer. "Garçon," he cried, "une bière, s'il vous plaît." The waiter promptly brought him a beer and then promptly disappeared. The wolf sipped his beer and delighted in the knowledge that if he were in the U.S.A. a waiter would be hovering with his check. When he had finished his beer and had his fill of cafe sitting, the wolf cried, "Garçon! L'addition!" But no waiter appeared with his check. Afternoon melted into night but still no waiter appeared. Finally the wolf went inside the cafe where he found the waiter playing cards with some friends.

moral:

Waiters, like cops, are never around when you need one.

CAFÉS

There are two sides to a typical village café: the sunny outdoor terrace where tourists sip coffees and Cokes and the dark, dingy inside bar where locals gather to talk and drink *pastis*. Prices bear this out. Drinks are cheaper at the bar than at an outdoor table. But unless you thrive on local atmosphere it is worth the premium to sit in the sun where you will be left undisturbed to nurse your drink and read your Herald Tribune. Stop by for breakfast but don't expect much beyond coffee and some bread. We once asked for croissants and the waiter had to walk up the street to a boulangerie to get some. Of course, larger cafés in larger towns have more to offer. Cafés serve light lunches, usually a plat du jour, salads, sandwiches and omelets. When you see a café that has some tables with tablecloths and some with-out, sit at one with a tablecloth if you're having a meal and sit at a bare table if you only want a snack or drink. At big, busy cafés you will usually pay when your order arrives. Other times you'll have to call the waiter (don't call him **garçon!**) when you're ready to settle up and leave.

Pastis,

the so-called "milk of Provence," is a potent anise-based liqueur that turns from amber to milky white when water is added. It is the descendant of the notorious *absinthe* which was banned in 1915. The major brands include Richard, Granier and Henri Bardouin. The last has a distillery you can visit in Forcalquier.

(actual size)

"un café"

Café noir or **express** is a very small cup of very strong coffee; an espresso. For a large cup of weaker coffee, order a **café américain**. **Café crème** is an espresso with warm, foamy milk (a latte). **Café au lait** is coffee with milk. For decaf coffee, order **déca**.

Beer (**bière**) comes in a variety of brands. **Pression** (draft) is cheaper than bottled.

A few other useful words

l'eau minerale	mineral water
avec gaz	sparkling
sans gaz	still
Croque monsieur	Toasted ham and cheese sandwich
Glace	ice cream
l'addition	check

Exploring the Luberon

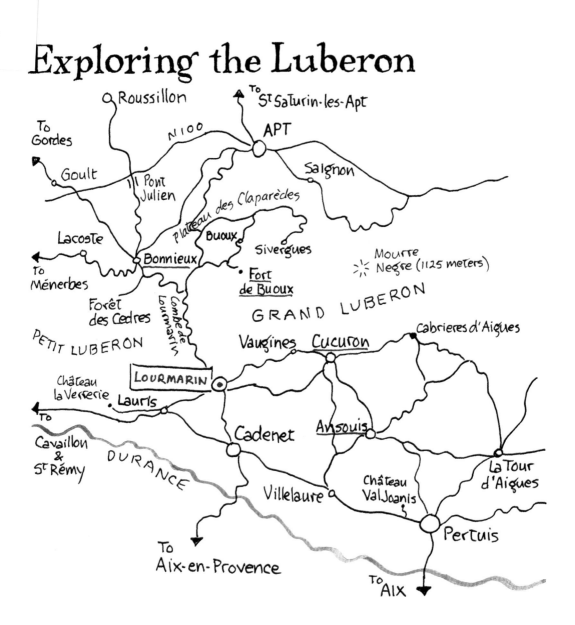

Roussillon

To St Saturin-les-Apt

To Gordes

N100

APT

Goult

Saignon

Pont Julien

Plateau des Claparèdes

Lacoste

Buoux

Sivergues

Mourre Negre (1125 meters)

Bonnieux

To Ménerbes

Fort de Buoux

GRAND LUBERON

Forêt des Cedres

Combe de Lourmarin

PETIT LUBERON

Cabrieres d'Aigues

Vaugines

Cucuron

Château la Verrerie

LOURMARIN

Lauris

To Cavaillon & St Rémy

Cadenet

Ansouis

La Tour d'Aigues

DURANCE

Villelaure

Château Val Joanis

To Aix-en-Provence

Pertuis

To AIX

Lourmarin sits in the heart of the Luberon, a region in Vaucluse that takes its name from the mountain range north of the Durance. The mountains consist of *le Petit Luberon* to the west and *le grand Luberon* to the east. A fault, the *Combe de Lourmarin*, divides the two. The Petit is topped by a beautiful forest of cedar trees you can access from the road to Bonnieux.

Atop the Combe to the east is the *Plateau des Claparèdes* with its scattered fields of lavender and dry-stone huts called *bories* and the bustling market town of Apt. On the southern side the landscape is less rugged and consists largely of vineyards (more about Côtes du Luberon wines later) and orchards. The towns and villages here are dedicated more to agriculture than tourism, but two, Ansouis and Cucuron, are worth a look.

Borie and lavender near Bonnieux

The largest town in the vicinity is scruffy Pertuis, which we visit only for its large supermarket (*Hyper-U*). On the outskirts is the winery Château Val Joanis which we do recommend for its formal gardens as well as its wines. Cadenet, another good-sized town, is one we just drive through on our way to Aix-en-Provence, a must-see city about 30 minutes from Lourmarin.

We have also rented a house near Lauris, just west of Lourmarin on the road to Cavaillon and the Alpilles. Just beyond Lauris on a back road is Château La Verrerie, our favorite wine of the region. It has a welcoming tasting room set among rows of lavender and olive trees.

The Luberon region is home to wonderful restaurants and hotels, from comfortable to luxurious. The colorful markets and shops sell regional foods and crafts, notably *santons*. There are plenty of trails for hiking and cafés for sitting. It's a part of Provence not to be missed.

A very short walking tour of

ANSOUIS

le château

Unless it's market day (Thursday), park in the lot next to the tabac. (There's an "only-if-necessary" W.C. under the lot) Head up rue du Petit Portail to reach the château. The first left leads to the studio of Daniel Galli, a santonnier. At the Mairie go under the arch and climb to Place du Château. Uphill past the Tourist Office is a gate that leads to the château. (The château changed hands in 2008 so its availability for tours is unknown). Grand Rue, to the left, leads to a cute ice cream/tea room (Les Moissines) and a broad view across the surrounding farms and vineyards. To return, take Rue du Cartel. You'll pass the clock tower (l'Horloge) and some attractive homes tucked among the walls. If it's between 2:00 and 6:00pm and you're in the mood for something different, when you reach the parking lot turn at the Sports Bar and go down a steep hill to the curious, but well-named, Musée Extraordinaire. Bring a sense of humor.

Market Day
Cucuron

The Essential CUCURON

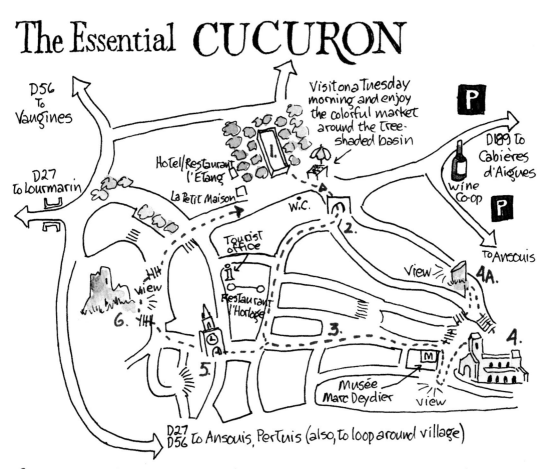

D56 To Vaugines

Visit on a Tuesday morning and enjoy the colorful market around the tree-shaded basin

P

D189 To Cabières d'Aigues

Hotel/Restaurant l'Etang

D27 To Lourmarin

La Petit Maison

Wine Co-op

P

W.C.

1.

2.

To Ansouis

Tourist office

View

4A.

Restaurant l'Horloge

View

4.

6. YHH

3.

5.

M

Musée Marc Deydier

View

D27 D56 To Ansouis, Pertuis (also, to loop around village)

Cucuron's most distinctive feature is **1.** the "étang", a raised basin surrounded by two rows of towering plane trees. Enter the interior at **2.** Portail de l'Etang. There's a little commercial hub **3.** Climb up to **4.** L'Eglise Notre Dame de Beaulieu. If you want a higher viewpoint, climb to the ruins of a tower **4A.** above the church. Pass under the arch of a 16th Century belfry **5.** and climb to the ruins of the 10th century Donjon Saint Michel. Cucuron is not much of a shopper's town. Restaurant l'Horloge is excellent. Enter from either of two streets.

Fort de Buoux is Les Baux without crowds. If you avoid weekends and holidays you'll probably find a parking spot in the fort's lot. From here a wide trail climbs gradually, passes under an imposing rock overhang and reaches a cute cottage where the "pay lady" tends her garden and collects a modest entry fee. The trail steepens and narrows to the *Porte d'Entrée*. You climb over rocks and walls

Fort de Buoux

This "undiscovered" find would be a favorite even if it weren't on the way to Auberge des Seguins

and the remains of guardrooms, cisterns, and "houses." There's a ruined church, more walls, trenches and steps and finally the watch tower at the top. The fort sits high on a rock spur, a natural defensive position if there ever was one. Before it was ordered destroyed by Louis XIV, it was inhabited by Ligurians, Romans, Catholics and Protestants, but so far, not by tourists.

Porte d'Entrée
Fort de Buoux

Lots of lavender and scattered bories in the hills around Buoux and Bonnieux

APT
Saignon
D232
D3
D113
Buoux
Sivergues
Bonnieux
D232
Auberge des Seguins
Fort de Buoux

Excellent alternate lunch stop if price is no object Auberge de L'Aiguebrun

D943
To Lourmarin
Careful! Tricky turn. Road to "town" of Buoux doubles back uphill, road to fort goes down

Auberge des Seguins sits at the end of the Fort Buoux road at the base of a colorful cliff. Park here and reserve for lunch. (Allow about two hours for the walk). Request the covered terrace. They serve good, simple food. The prix fixe menu includes a platter of varied hors d'oeuvre, a plat (the trout is excellent, as is the lamb stew), salad and choice of desserts. Wine by the pitcher or bottle.

A favorite walk and lunch*

The round trip to Sivergues offers two very different walks, both easy. The first climbs in the open with views across the valley and is more road than trail. The route back is all trail and follows the creek (L'Aigue Brun) through a forest of vines and cliffs.

Leave the Seguins parking area, cross the bridge and take the road uphill to the left and follow signs for "Sivergues." You'll pass two bories (stone huts) and, further on, some troglodyte buildings.

Enjoy the little chapel and few buildings that comprise Sivergues, but don't plan on finding a bathroom or cold drink.

At the foot of the village look for sign posts for "L'Aigue Brun" and "Les Seguins." It's your path back to lunch.

Bonnieux

Like many *villages perchés*, Bonnieux is prettiest when viewed from afar, either coming down from Lourmarin or up from Lacoste. The road that winds through town is narrow and the side streets are steep. There is an old church with good views at the top of town. For a good mid-way starting point, look for a parking place along the low wall overlooking the newer church at the bottom of town. From here you can enjoy the view of Lacoste, then walk up to a few shops and a favorite art gallery of ours, *Galerie Janin-Ruggeri*. Around the corner from the Hotel César (where you can sit on the tiny terrace and watch tour buses squeeze by) you'll find the *Musée de la Boulangerie* with more than you need to know about bread-baking.

Climb up to the old church or go back to a pedestrian switchback that leads down to a tiny square with a fountain. Here you'll find the tourist office and an excellent restaurant, *Le Fournil*. Across the street and down another level is the Place Gambetta where Bonnieux's Friday morning market is held.

To avoid this severe switchback, drivers to Lourmarin are directed LEFT, toward Apt and a roundabout that will point them back in the right direction

La Bastide de la Capelonge (Pricey hotel & Restaurant)

To Lourmarin

Upper Church

Great views

Mairie

long climb

Musée de la Boulangerie

Street Parking (Good view)

Tourist Office

To APT

Restaurant Le Fournil

Hotel César

Galerie Janin-Ruggerie

Pedestrian switchback

To Roussillon

Lower Church

Place Gambetta

To Lacoste & Ménerbes

Walking Tour

A Provence Fable

The crow's bright idea

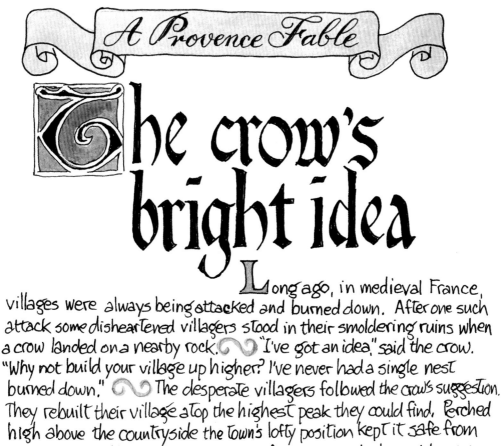

Long ago, in medieval France, villages were always being attacked and burned down. After one such attack some disheartened villagers stood in their smoldering ruins when a crow landed on a nearby rock. "I've got an idea," said the crow. "Why not build your village up higher? I've never had a single nest burned down." The desperate villagers followed the crow's suggestion. They rebuilt their village atop the highest peak they could find. Perched high above the countryside the town's lofty position kept it safe from attack. Unfortunately, except for crows, nobody could get to or from the village, which eventually fell into disrepair.

moral:

The "village perché" seemed like a good idea at the time.

A full day of hill towns

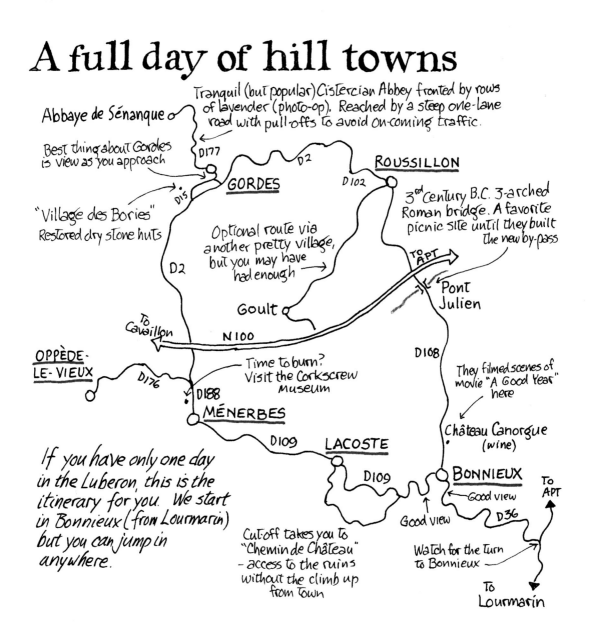

Abbaye de Sénanque

Tranquil (but popular) Cistercian Abbey fronted by rows of lavender (photo-op). Reached by a steep one-lane road with pull-offs to avoid on-coming traffic.

Best thing about Gordes is view as you approach

D177

D2

ROUSSILLON

D102

GORDES

D15

"Village des Bories" Restored dry stone huts

3rd Century B.C. 3-arched Roman bridge. A favorite picnic site until they built the new by-pass

Optional route via another pretty village, but you may have had enough

D2

TO APT

Pont Julien

Goult

To Cavaillon

N100

D168

OPPÈDE-LE-VIEUX

D176

Time to burn? Visit the Corkscrew Museum

They filmed scenes of movie "A Good Year" here

D188

MÉNERBES

Château Canorgue (wine)

D109

LACOSTE

If you have only one day in the Luberon, this is the itinerary for you. We start in Bonnieux (from Lourmarin) but you can jump in anywhere.

D109

BONNIEUX

TO APT

Good view

Good view

D36

Cut-off takes you to "Chemin de Château" - access to the ruins without the climb up from Town

Watch for the Turn to Bonnieux

To Lourmarin

Lacoste

    The main attraction of Lacoste is
that for 30 years it was the home of the notorious Marquis de Sade. His château,
whose ruins look down on this hilltop town, was destroyed during the
Revolution while its owner was imprisoned in Paris.

    The town has slicked up in recent years with the addition of a few new
restaurants and galleries, the latter probably due to the presence of an American
school run by the Cleveland Institute of Art. The best place to park to visit the
village is in a small square by the Post Office. (There's also a W.C. there.) The
streets are steep and narrow.

Oppède-le-Vieux

Park in the lot *(payant)* and follow a path through terraced gardens to the "new" village of restored homes and a couple of cafés. From the square go through a gateway in the wall and climb to the upper village. The path is rough and steep in places. You'll pass overgrown ruins, finally reaching a 13th century church and the ruins of a château, home of the infamous Baron d'Oppède who led the massacre of the Waldenses in 1545.

MÉNERBES

Ménerbes is one of those quaint Luberon villages that owe their current popularity (ruination?) to Peter Mayle. It is a long village. Park, if you can, in the small lot next to the terrace of the Bar du Progrès and Restaurant Clémentine, both nice stops for lunch with a view. There are a few small shops nearby, but to see the sights walk past Café du Progrès and climb to the Town Hall and 14th century church. Walk through the cemetery and look down on le Castellet, a small 15th century castle owned by the widow of artist Nicholas de Stael.

Actually a come-on to the tasting/sales room of Domaine de la Citadelle (pretty good wine) the corkscrew museum has over 1000 pieces from the 17th century to the present, some playfully erotic

Musée du-Tire Bouchon

Musée du Tire-Bouchon

M ─ D3

Oppède-le-Vieux ○ ─ D188 ─ Ménerbes ─ D103 ─ D106 ─ Abbey St Hillaire ─ D109 ─ Lacoste ─ ○ Bonnieux

D3

GORDES

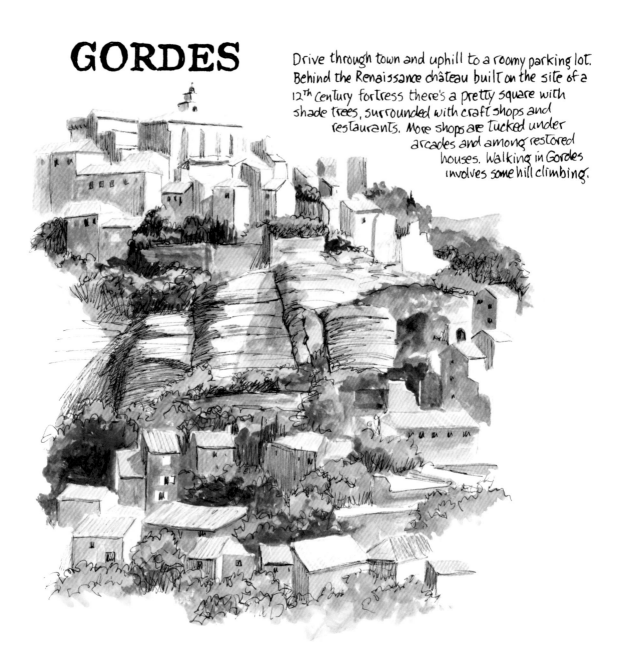

Drive through town and uphill to a roomy parking lot. Behind the Renaissance château built on the site of a 12th Century fortress there's a pretty square with shade trees, surrounded with craft shops and restaurants. More shops are tucked under arcades and among restored houses. Walking in Gordes involves some hill climbing.

ROUSSILLON

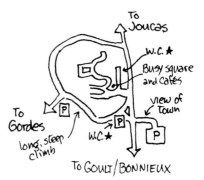

Orange, yellow and red buildings made from the ochre clay mined here give the town a uniquely colorful appearance. There are lots of shops and galleries, and as a result, lots of visitors.

Driving from Gordes you are invited to park below the town. To avoid a steep climb, drive up and around and try for a small lot at the top. If this is filled there's a big upper lot with the bonus of a great view of town. Follow the crowds past shops to a pretty square with many cafés. Continue up and under the arch of a picturesque bell tower. Panoramic view at the top of town.

A LOOK AT LAVENDER

Sault — Hosts a lavender fair in Aug. Whole town has faint scent of lavender

Revest du Brion

Heaviest concentration of lavender

Quiet town with new church at bottom, old church at top, good views in between. Noted for its leaf-wrapped chèvre (goat cheese)

St Christol

Banon

Simiane-la-Rotonde

D50

D950

Alternate route if you opt to skip Forcalquier

Carniol

Narrow winding roads

Revest-des-Brousse

Forcalquier

To **Rustrel & "Colorado,"** a region of ochre cliffs popular with hikers

Oppedette — Magnificently sited collection of ruins and restoration projects

St Michel l'Observatoire

Viens

Reillane

D14

St Martin de Castillon

Cereste

N 100

As you approach town take the [P] turn to the left. It seems too soon to park, but by the time you reach the lot you'll be right below the town center. Town is a nice blend of new (services) and old (character). Old town winds up-hill behind church, which sits on main square ringed with cafés. There's also a pastis distillery you can visit.

Simiane-la-Rotonde sits high on plateau dominated by remains of feudal castle that resembles a huge overturned pail of wet sand. Interior can be visited. Town has picturesque covered market place with view over the plain.

Two perched villages connected by a spectacular drive

It's hard to drive through Provence without seeing neat rows of lavender, but the countryside between Banon and Sault is especially rich with it.

FacToid: It takes 120-130 kilos of lavender flowers and stems to make one kilo of lavender essence.

Unless you're here in late June or July you'll have to imagine the rows of grey hedgehogs as the sea of purple you see on postcards.

The pig who went to market

A pig who loved food looked forward to her first trip to a provençal market. She loved to stroll through the stands of olives, cherries and white asparagus. She brought her big straw market basket. ∽ "Where to start?" she wondered when she arrived. First she bought some plump, juicy strawberries and put them in the bottom of her basket. Next she bought apples, beans and a small bag of potatoes. ∽ "Oooh! Lavender honey!" She bought a big jar and a crock of herbes de Provence, then two bottles of wine. ∽ "Enough!" she thought. "This basket is getting heavy." As she headed home with her loaded basket she noticed a dog following her, eagerly licking up dripping strawberry juice.

moral:

Even a short trip requires careful packing.

Outdoor Markets

There is an outdoor market somewhere in Provence every day of the week. They range from a few vans that show up in the village square to the sprawling food and antiques extravaganza at L'Isle-sur-la-Sorgue.

You'll find colorful provençal fabrics and flowers, fresh fruits and vegetables, clothes and jewelry, pottery and crafts and, usually, a man with a goat, selling cough drops.

We tend to end up with the following items in our market basket: a wedge of mountain cheese (after a sample has been sliced from a big wheel and urged on us by persistent sellers), lavender honey (a variety of flavors are set out with little wooden spoons for tasting), white asparagus (on its way out of season by May, but still good), cherries (on their way in by May, and fantastic), strawberries (red all the way through), herbes de Provence, lettuce, tomatoes, a bouquet of flowers and a rotisserie chicken with a scoop of potatoes and juice droppings.

Our favorite markets

MONDAY LUNDI
Cadenet

TUESDAY MARDI
Cucuron

WEDNESDAY MERCREDI
St. Rémy

THURSDAY JEUDI
Aix-en-Provence

FRIDAY VENDREDI
Lourmarin

SATURDAY SAMEDI
Apt

SUNDAY DIMANCHE
L'Isle-sur-la-Sorgue

HOW TO ORDER

That one
Ce (or) là

A little
un peu

This much.

a. A bit more
plus
b. A bit less
moins

Whoa!
Enough!

A few more useful words of French

Je voudrais des____ I would like some —

Une tranche   A slice
Un morceau   A piece
Combien   How much?
Acceptez-vous Visa? (not recommended)

Level Three
MOST
FRAGILE

Level Two
MODERATE

Level One
HEAVIEST

Herbes
de
Provence

Rookie   Veteran

HOW TO PACK YOUR MARKET BASKET

Heavy stuff on the bottom; light, fragile stuff on top. Unfortunately, this is opposite of how you'd like to shop, buying light things first and heavier items last

Sunday in L'Isle-Sur-La-Sorgue

This is the mother of all markets. The riverside setting and the addition of antiques and *brocante* on Sunday make this market worth a visit, despite the crowds. Café de France in the center of town is a popular spot to rest with a coffee. Lots of antique shops are tucked away in courtyards. Go early and park at your first opportunity.

Our favorite route to market is the D31 from Robion

SORGUE

To AVIGNON

D31

N100

Fontaine-de-Vaucluse (source of river)

D22

Cavaillon

Robion

N100 To Apt & Bonnieux

Market Day
L'Isle-sur-la-Sorgue

Supermarkets

The picturesque outdoor market will always be the romantic way to buy food, but for no-nonsense stockup shopping you can't beat the **supermarché** It's like home, with differences.

First, you "rent" your cart in the parking lot. Deposit a Euro coin to unlock a cart and when you return, plug it into the cart ahead and get your coin back. Good idea, n'est-ce pas?

Inside, once you've pushed through the aisles of clothing, hardware and outdoor furniture and entered the world of groceries, it feels more familiar. Except everything has a different name. You'll recognize some international brands like Kellogg's and Nestlé, but there's a dazzling array of new faces. Canned cassoulet (Joan's favorite), pre-made sauces like béchamel, beurre blanc and hollandaise. There's crème fraîche, fois gras and fresh pasta, plus many, many cheeses.

When it comes to fresh produce, you have to do some work before you reach the checkout. Pick out and bag what you want. If it's sold by weight, put your bag on the scales, select the matching picture and push the button. Out comes a price sticker to affix to your bag.

The wine section is like a trip through the vineyards of France. It's very tempting, but we still prefer to visit the wineries themselves.

When you get to the checkout lanes (Surprise! Not all 25 are open) don't expect much help. You have to bag your own groceries (in bags you have to bring!) and tote the bags to your car. But that's okay, because you want to get your coin back for your cart.

Don't forget to bring your own shopping bag!

The Joy of Cooking

Basil

I buy a plant in a pot at the supermarket and keep it inside and pick leaves as needed for tomatoes, salads, pasta, fruit

Cooking in Provence is more enjoyable than cooking at home. Maybe it's the ingredients, fresh from the market. Maybe it's the new "convenience" foods from the Super-U. Maybe it's having the time to experiment in my "own" farmhouse kitchen.

Breakfast is easy. Yesterday's baguette, sliced, toasted and slathered with lavender honey, cherry preserves or quince jelly. Fresh-squeezed orange juice. Perhaps a slice of Cavaillon melon or fresh strawberries. Sometimes eggs scrambled with crème fraîche and lardons.

Lunch, at home or from a picnic basket, is a fresh crusty baguette with some cheeses, ham, rillettes, paté, leftover chicken, fruit and "school boys" (cookies). And, of course, wine.

Dinners are more creative. Here are some ideas:

salade frisée

Sauté lardons (smoked bacon), then toss croutons into lardon oil. Add to frisé greens and toss with vinaigrette. Serve with poached egg on top. Just like in a bistrot.

Lamb

Buy a whole leg of lamb at a boucherie. Roast with salt, pepper, olive oil and *herbes de Provence* for 4 hours. Start high and lower heat when outside is crispy.

Fish

A simple grilled dorade or sole may look daunting when you see it staring up from the fish counter. Just ask the man to prepare it. He will clean it for you. Then just sauté or grill and finish with lemon and a beurre blanc sauce.

VEAL

Buy a veal shoulder. Cube, sauté in oil, add peppers, onions and wine (red or white), then bake slowly 2 hours. Serve over rice.

A favorite meal!
Rub chicken with lemon, olive oil, salt, pepper & herbes de Provence. Put squeezed lemons into chicken cavity. Roast 2 hours or until crispy brown. Serve with a chilled Tavel.

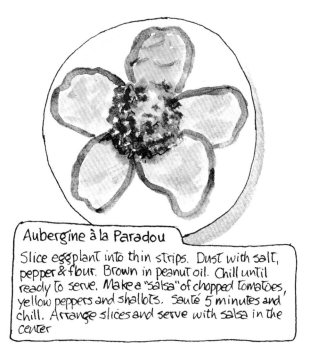

Aubergine à la Paradou

Slice eggplant into thin strips. Dust with salt, pepper & flour. Brown in peanut oil. Chill until ready to serve. Make a "salsa" of chopped tomatoes, yellow peppers and shallots. Sauté 5 minutes and chill. Arrange slices and serve with salsa in the center

Here's a dish inspired by Jardin de Frédéric in St Rémy. Peel & cook asparagus. Cut feuilleté (puff pastry) sheet into rectangles to fit 4 or 5 spears. Bake pastry per pkg. directions. Place asparagus on top and cover with beurre blanc sauce (purchased pre-made, but I doctor with a little crème fraiche.

Cassoulet
de Castelnaudary

au Canard

+

Raynel et Roquelaure

PROVENÇAL COOKING, SIMPLIFIED

There's nothing like home cooking to relieve the expense of restaurant dining. And there's nothing like prepared, packaged supermarket foods to make home cooking easy.

Joan's favorite recipe. Open can, heat and serve.

Rotisserie chickens available at any outdoor market, ready for dinner or a fancy picnic

We praised the chef at Domaine de Cabasse for his fresh ravioli, then found this at the supermarket. Refrigerated pasta. Boil for one minute. Add olive oil, chopped basil and grated emmenthaler cheese.

RAVIOLES
du Dauphine

Pots de crème. La laitière brand from Nestlé. Great crème caramel.

DESSERT IDEA

Drive to Cavaillon. Buy melon. Drive to Beaumes-de-Venise. Buy bottle of Muscat. Combine & chill

CARTE D'OR
The name to look for for ice cream.

EASY TART

Put whole round of feuilleté in pastry dish. Bake until fluffy and brown. Fill with strawberries and cover with strawberry preserves which have been boiled and strained.

Herbes de Provence
Illustrated

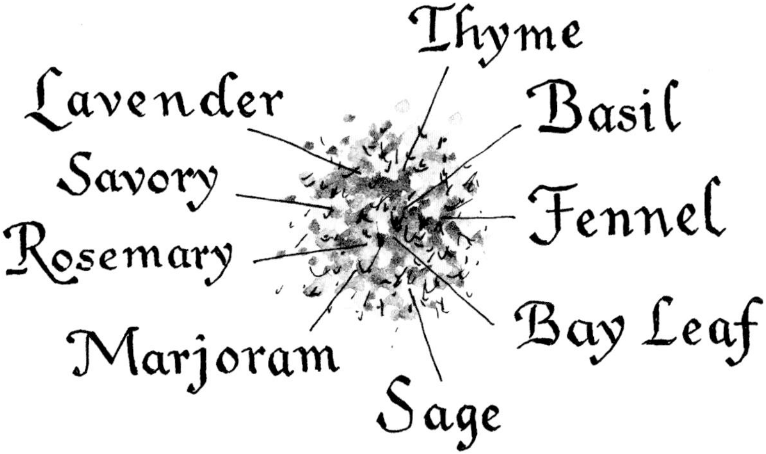

Thyme

Lavender

Basil

Savory

Fennel

Rosemary

Bay Leaf

Marjoram

Sage

You'll find them at every market and souvenir shop in cellophane bags or cute earthenware pots. They are to the nose what a field of poppies or lavender is to the eye -- an indelible memory of Provence. Herbes de Provence add the flavor of the region to roast chicken, lamb, chèvre, omelettes fine herbes, grilled pork, fresh tomatoes in olive oil, rabbit, asparagus or a simple bistro-style steak frites.

THE COMPLEAT
BAGUETTE

Baguettes are baked fresh twice daily and for good reason. Buy your lunch bread in the morning and your dinner loaf in the afternoon. By morning it will be good only for toast. Buy them at a Boulangerie. If your town has more than one, choose the one with the longer line. Locals know their pain. Try to avoid supermarket baguettes wrapped in cellophane.

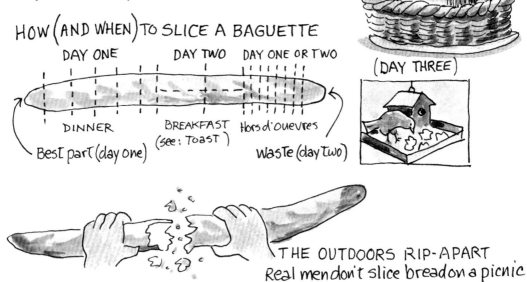

HOW (AND WHEN) TO SLICE A BAGUETTE

DAY ONE DAY TWO DAY ONE OR TWO

DINNER   BREAKFAST Hors d'ouevres
     (see: Toast)

Best part (day one)   Waste (day two)

(DAY THREE)

THE OUTDOORS RIP-APART
Real men don't slice bread on a picnic

How to wrap a baguette

a. → b.

1. Cut tissue to size of average human hand
2. Fold over sides a. and b. and tape (basic) or knot (advanced)

Add tapenade for an easy hors d'oueuvre

For more bread info visit the Musée de la Boulangerie in Bonnieux

How to carry a baguette

or

Are you glad to see me or have you been to the boulangerie?

TOAST

Cut yesterday's baguette into 4 inch segments. Slice segments lengthwise. Toast. Scrape off burnt edges. Add butter and lavender honey or preserves (confiture).

BASIC LOAVES

BAGUETTE
Ubiquitous loaf of variable length, thickness and quality

L'ANCIENNE
Thinner and crustier, as the name suggests

RESTAURANT
Oversize baguette for groups or big appetites

ÉPI
Pull-apart into "rolls". More crust per loaf

The Tortoise & the hare

Once upon a time there was a tortoise who ran a restaurant in the south of France. The food was good but the service was, predictably, slow. Even a simple lunch took two hours. ⌇ One day a hare opened a restaurant across the street and challenged the tortoise to a race. ⌇ "Let's see who can get customers in and out faster," said the hare. The tortoise reluctantly agreed and at noon sharp they were off! The hare raced to the kitchen with orders and sped back with entrées. The tortoise plodded along as usual. As he crept back with a tray of entrées, the speedy hare was already taking dessert orders. But sensing he was ahead, the hare took his time with the coffees. ⌇ And everybody's check arrived at the same time.

moral:

A restaurant meal takes two hours. Period.

Eating Out

When we are in Provence we seem to spend an increasing amount of time wondering where our next meal is coming from. The quest begins anytime after breakfast (petit déjeuner), which is not the big meal it is in America. Serious eating does not begin until noon.

If we are in a big, busy town (or if we know in advance the restaurant we'd like to try) we find our choice in the morning and make a reservation. We base our decision on ambience, price and menu. There is no excuse for being surprised by price or selection because every restaurant posts its menu outside. (You also feel less self-conscious consulting your menu translator while standing on the sidewalk than seated at your table.)

Look first at le menu, a prix-fixe selection of appetizer, main dish (plat) and dessert. There are often several to choose from with different prices. No substitutions. If you can't find a *menu* you want you can order à la carte. You'll pay more, often a lot more, but it is your meal so order what you want.

Somewhere on the menu (carte) it may tell you whether or not service is included. It usually is. Service compris means it is, but you may want to leave a few coins more. Service non compris, or s.n.c., means that you are expected to tip. When you do, 15% is sufficient.

A typical meal out will include a starter, a main dish, then cheese and/or dessert. Coffee is ordered <u>after</u> dessert. One of the longest waits you're likely to encounter is between coffee and the check (l'addition). We Americans tend to arrive "early" (7:30 to 8:00), so when we've finished and are trying to catch the waiter's eye, he's busy with local diners who arrived at 8:30 or 9 o'clock.

Although it takes a big chunk out of a day of touring, we prefer to make lunch the big meal of the day. For one thing, it's cheaper than dinner. Plus, if the weather is nice you can usually eat outdoors. Restaurants start serving lunch at noon, get a bit sullen by 1:30 and stop seating at 2:00.

Don't be surprised if one of the diners at the next table is a dog.

TIPS FOR DINING OUT

1. Any meal tastes better eaten outdoors.
2. Avoid any restaurant with an illustrated menu. (Exception: ice cream sundaes)
3. Be grateful for, but suspicious of, a menu written in English.
4. Go with the *plat du jour*.
5. Order a *menu*, not à la carte.
6. Try regional or house specialties.
7. The better the restaurant, the better the chance the beef will be tender.
8. When in doubt, order chicken.
9. Don't expect to eat and run.

There are different types of eating establishments for different occasions and appetites. At the top of the food chain is le restaurant. A restaurant serves meals, not snacks. They don't understand, "I'd like just a salad." They offer complete prix fixe menus as well as à la carte, but you're expected to order a full meal. They are open for lunch and dinner, sometimes just dinner, and you should expect to spend at least two hours at table. For lighter, more casual dining, look for un café. Cafes are open all day and you can order just a drink or choose from a limited selection of snacks, sandwiches, salads and such. They usually have some sort of outdoor terrace. Some larger, more ambitious ones bill themselves as café-restaurant. They will have some tables with table cloths for those ordering a full meal. Again, check the posted menu. Un bar is where you go for a drink (not coffee). Un bistro is usually a small, less formal, less expensive restaurant. Une brasserie is a hybrid restaurant/cafe, likely to offer faster service and more flexible hours. Un salon de thé is an informal tea room/coffeehouse offering pastries and desserts. Une buvette is a kiosk or roadside stand serving cold drinks and snacks. *Bon appétit!*

Missing something? "Je voudrais _____"

du sel

du pain

Les verres (pour le vin)   (pour l'eau)

une tasse

du sucre

du poivre

une serviette

un couteau

une fourchette

Une assiette

une cuillere

The man who ate Brains

A couple who spoke very good English but not very good French stopped for lunch one day. They chose a bistrot offering *poulet*, a french word they knew meant chicken. They sat down and in their best French ordered, "Poulet." "Pas de poulet," said the waiter. "Cervelles." "Whatever," said the couple, pleased that the conversation was going as well as it was. When the waiter returned he had plates of what any biology student would recognize as brains, on rice, covered with gray gravy. Later, as the waiter removed their barely touched plates, he inquired, "Dessert?" "Oui," said the still hungry couple. "Pruneaux ou glace?" "Glace," they guessed, luckily avoiding their first ever lunch of brains and prunes.

moral:

When dining out
in France, it helps to know a word or two of French.

May we recommend...

We've found the following to be good bets. (If your tastes run to bouillabaisse and sweetbreads you're on your own.)

Soupe au pistou is a hearty minestrone with basil and garlic, almost a meal in itself. Soupe de poissons (fish soup) is not for everyone, but can be delicious. It's served with large croutons, aioli (garlic mayonnaise) and grated cheese and tastes its best at a seaside restaurant. Another good regional starter is caillette, a terrine of ground pork sausage with spinach. (Not to be confused in your menu translator with caille (quail).

The fish we look for is dorade (sea bream), a mild white fish that is excellent grilled and usually served head and all. Loup de mer (Mediterranean sea bass) is another good choice, but it's more dependent on the sauce that accompanies it.

For meat, seek out l'agneau de Sisteron (lamb from Sisteron) in any of a variety of forms: carré d'agneau (ribs or loin) gigot (leg) épaule (shoulder) or côte d'agneau (chop). Do not ask for mint jelly.

Auberge des Seguins makes a tasty estouffade (lamb stew with black olives), but in Provence stew means daube. A slow-cooked daube de boeuf is one of the best ways to have beef, which can be tough and disappointing, except in finer restaurants. Poulet (chicken) is always a safe bet, always delicious. Poulet roti (roast chicken) with frites (french fries) is a favorite lunch.

FRITES! We don't call them <u>french</u> fries for nothing.

For a regional twist look for chicken in lavender sauce. You should also try lapin (rabbit) if you see it on the menu (especially at Bistrot du Paradou). Our daughter, then seven, ate rabbit and declared, "This chicken tastes just like home."

Except for fromage blanc it's hard to go wrong at dessert. Tarte de _____ (any seasonal fruit) is a good choice and the ice cream (glace) is excellent, but nobody understands "à la mode."

How would you like your meat?
bleu Barely warm saignant rare (no need to specify)
rosé medium rare à point medium bien cuit well-done (be prepared to defend your choice)

The Gourmet's Last Wish

A gourmet in search of the perfect meal sat in a restaurant one night when a genie appeared and offered him two wishes. "Not three?" asked the gourmet ∽ "Don't be a pig," said the genie. The gourmet eyed the promising menu and wished aloud for the *charlotte de foie gras* to start. It appeared in a poof and tasted sublime. But the *côte de boeuf* that followed was disappointing. ∽ "I wish I could get a main dish as good as that starter," said the gourmet. POOF! The genie served him a *pigeoneau rôti à la broche* that took his breath away. But the dessert that followed was sadly uninspired. ∽ "Just once," said the frustrated gourmet, "I wish I could have a meal in which every course was perfect. ∽ "Sorry," huffed the angry genie. "Two wishes only!" And he disappeared.

moral:

With any three-course restaurant meal
one or two great courses are all you can wish for.

The Impossible Dream

The perfect restaurant meal combines to-die-for food, impeccable service and charming ambience, all at a bargain price. Sadly, such a meal does not exist. Still, the search can be fun. If you bring modest expectations to the table you are more likely to be pleasantly surprised. If you go to a Michelin 3-star you are waiting to be impressed, looking for flaws, daring the food to live up to its prices. Try a top-rated restaurant some time, but approach it as theater. Very often it is the little out-of-the-way place you stumble upon that will have the meal you most remember. This does not mean that every grubby eatery harbors a great meal, nor that every gourmet restaurant is destined to disappoint. Two people at the same table can have different reactions depending upon what each orders. Sometimes an appetizer may dazzle you and the entree be just so-so. But a truly bad meal is hard to find in Provence.

DINNER AS THEATER
La Bastide de Marie

Joan's pistachio ice cream with strawberry coulis was served with two sprigs of génet. When we said we'd heard that génet was poisonous the waiter assured us it was fine as long as she didn't eat it.

My starter

Ivy (inedible)
Mussels
Beans
Soup

The soup was to search for!

A TALE OF TWO LUNCHES

Auberge de l'Aiguebrun

Down a rough dirt road off the D943 between Lourmarin and Apt is the Auberge de l'Aiguebrun, a beautiful country inn and restaurant. A sunny glassed-in dining room overlooks a terrace and gardens bordering the Aiguebrun. Très élegant! Prix fixe menu with three choices per course. Our choices: asparagus salad topped with a soft boiled egg. Artichokes stewed in broth. Both superb as only perfectly prepared fresh vegetables can be. These followed an "amuse bouche" - a miniature cup of fish soup with mousseline. Entrées: loup with zucchini "spaghetti," and rabbit with mushrooms. For dessert we chose gâteau chocolat en crème anglais. A 1995 Vacqueyras, mineral water and coffees. L'addition: don't ask.

RESTAURANT "LE LISERON"

Just when we thought nothing was open in Lambesc, we spotted "Le Liseron". It was not only open, it was packed, and everyone seemed to be eating the same thing. It was the *plat du jour* and we joined in. A green salad with artichokes followed by a slab of roast pork with buttered noodles. Desserts - a flourless nut cake with chocolat sauce and an *Ile flotant* -- meringue floating in crème anglais. By the time we had finished we were alone in the room. The chef, dressed in last week's dirty whites, came out of the kitchen and chatted with us. A bottle of Côtes du Rhone Villages and coffees. Delicious - and reasonable!

Two completely different, but equally satisfying dining experiences. One a stumble-upon local restaurant, the other a highly recommended country auberge with grand cuisine.
Ya pays yer money and takes yer choice.

The Little Redfaced Hen

One day a mother hen decided to take her chicks on a special outing. ∾ "Today we're going to visit an historic château," she told them. But it was Tuesday and the château was closed on Tuesdays. ∾ "No matter," she chirped. "We'll go on a picnic." ∾ But by the time they found a grocery store it was 12:30 and the store was closed. ∾ "No problem. We'll have lunch at a pretty country restaurant," she chirped. Alas, the restaurant she took them to had closed for the season. ∾ One of her chicks piped up, "I know a place that's always open." So they all went to America.

moral:

In Provence, nothing is always open.

Shopping for a picnic
(A cautionary tale)

How many times must one learn the same lesson? Do not wait until noon to go shopping in Provence. Even if the task is as simple as, "Don't forget to pick up a bottle of wine."

I was sketching around Lacoste while Joan guided visiting friends on a morning of sightseeing. She would buy a baguette at the Cucuron market and we'd meet at Pont Julien for a picnic at 1 p.m. All I had to do was remember to buy wine.

At 11:50 I realized I'd forgotten. The nearest wine was at the *Musée de Tire-Bouchon* at Domaine de la Citadelle, a winery near Ménerbes. Tuesday is never a good day to plan to visit a museum, even one connected to the domaine's tasting and sales room. Predictably, it was closed. It was now 12:30 and only Ménerbes lay between me and an embarrassingly dry picnic.

I spun uphill to the village. Amazingly, the Epicerie was still open. But by the time I had parked and hurried back it was being shuttered. My gasp must have been audible because the woman stopped closing up and looked at me. "Une bouteille du vin?" I implored. "Pour un pique-nique?" She pushed the door open and I grabbed the nearest bottle, ironically, a Domaine de la Citadelle. It tasted very good with cheese and cold chicken in the shadow of a 2000-year old Roman bridge.

It would have tasted even better if Joan had remembered to buy bread.

A Lament for Pont Julien

Until recently, when you drove from Roussillon to Bonnieux on the D149, you crossed the Coulon River on a narrow, one-lane stone bridge. It's called Pont Julien and it was built by the Romans in the 3rd Century B.C. It was a favorite picnic site.

Lately though, someone decided that the next thousand years pose a greater risk than the previous thousands, so they built a new bridge just upstream and installed a big roundabout to divert traffic, turning Pont Julien into a quaint relic to be glimpsed as you whiz by.

You can still picnic nearby but much of the charm and the sense of discovery is gone.

Apologies
to E. Manet

A Provence Fable

The Ant's Ideal Picnic

One sunny day some ants decided to go on a picnic. They all set out to find the ideal spot ∞ "There's one!" shouted an ant when he spied a family eating beside their car. ∞ "Too close to the road," said one very picky ant. So they moved on. ∞ "How about there?" asked another ant, pointing to a couple enjoying bread and cheese next to a creek. ∞ "Too sunny," said the picky ant. So they moved on. ∞ "There's a perfect spot!" said another ant pointing to a family lunching under a shady tree overlooking a vineyard. They all agreed that it looked good, but the picky ant said, "I'm just gonna check out that spot on the other side of the road." But as he started across the road the picky ant was flattened by a speeding car.

moral:

The ideal picnic spot is always just around the next bend.

Déjeuner sur l'herbe

A picnic is a great way to enjoy the provençal countryside (and stretch your meal budget). It can be simple or elaborate. Once, while picnicking near Pont-du-Gard, we watched a couple heat sauce for their lunch over a small gas burner.

Sponteneity is fun, but remember you can't suddenly decide at noon to have a picnic. Stores will be closing. Stock up in advance. You

can usually find everything you need at an outdoor market. Otherwise, go from store to store: a boulangerie for your bread, patisserie for a fancy dessert, charcuterie for sausages and patés, alimentation (grocery store) for vegetables, fruit, cheese and beverages. Speaking of beverages, if you're planning a long drive after lunch

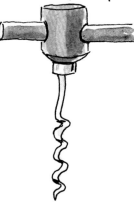

you may want to rethink the wine. Still, it is Provence and it is a picnic and a nice chilled rosé somehow completes the image.

SITE SELECTION. Face it, no picnic site you settle on will be quite as good as the one you passed a few miles earlier or the one you'll see just down the road. And remember, you're new here. The locals know where the best spots are. If it's scenic and accessible, chances are someone will already be there. But since their picnics tend to be elaborate affairs with tables and chairs, the farther from your car you're willing to walk, the more likely you are to find a secluded spot for lunch.

(MOIST TOWELETTE

Picnic Essentials

Wine. Better if your after-lunch plans feature a long nap, not a long drive.

Good! Someone remembered a corkscrew

Mineral water For drinking and cleaning up

Variety of cheeses. Chèvre and any other kind you can imagine. Don't forget a knife & cutting board

Fresh baguette Absolute must!

Fruit tart or other dessert from patisserie

Terrine or country paté from market or charcuterie

Mustard

evian

CÔTES DU RHONE

RILLETTES

MOUTARD

A real wine glass adds a touch of class, but an empty yogurt jar will work

Olives

Don't tell your heart doctor about this treat. Essentially animal fat. Ymmm!

Vegetables, if you insist

Apple or other fresh fruit

Cherries, picked off nearby tree if you're lucky (and discreet)

A Spectator's Guide to
Boules
A.K.A. *pétanque*

You will see this sport played on any available patch of gravel (*terraine de pétanque*). One team member tosses the cork (*cochonnet*), then throws one of his three boules, trying to get as close as he can to the cork. His opponent then throws, trying to place his closer. For each of its boules closer to the cork than an opponent's closest boule a team scores one point. A game consists of 13 points.

If it were that simple it wouldn't be so popular. It's all about technique (high arching shots, back-spin, etc.), strategy (knocking away an opponent's boule, throwing at the cork, etc.) and measuring. Plus lots of kibitzing and arguing.

The colors
of Provence

Poppies (les Coquelicots)

Gênet

The Fox & the Grapes

A fox who loved fine wine hated to pay fine wine prices. One day he saw people with big plastic jugs leaving the local wine co-op. He looked inside and saw wine being pumped from huge vats, like gasoline. "How much?" he asked. The fox couldn't believe his ears. It worked out to about $2 a bottle. The fox bought an empty jug and said, "Fill 'er up with rouge!" He could hardly wait to get home and taste it. He poured himself a glass and took a sip. He used the rest of his wine for cooking.

moral:

You get what you pay for.

Wines of Provence

A couple we'd invited to our rental house for dinner arrived with a bottle of wine and a fancy boxed pastry. Wine is a traditional hostess gift but the pastry seemed excessive. They explained that they had stopped at the local co-op and asked for their best bottle. When it turned out to cost three bucks they figured they had better bring a pastry, too.

Welcome to Provence, land of affordable wines.

Wine bottled or pumped from vats and sold en vrac (in plastic jugs) at co-ops is temptingly cheap. In the Luberon coops process about 90% of the grapes. These wines are less expensive than château bottled wines. But life is short (and vacations even shorter) and there are too many châteaux offering better wines at reasonable prices. Go for it.

The heart of Provence consists of three appellations: Côtes du Luberon, Coteaux d'Aix-en-Provence and Coteaux-des-Baux-de-Provence. You could drink very happily on just wines from these regions. But even better wines lie a short distance away. To the south are Cassis (excellent whites) and Bandol (red and rosé). And to the north are the famous Rhône wines: Gigondas, Vacqueyras, Beaumes-de-Venise (noted for their sweet muscat) and Châteauneuf-de-Pape. All these places are worth a visit even if you don't drink wine. Rosé is one of the pleasant surprises of the region. Quality ranges from pink vin ordinaire served by the glass in cafes to the proud wines of Lirac and Tavel.

If you are fortunate you may stumble across a Fête du Vin. Producers from a region assemble and set up booths for tasting. You buy a glass and walk from booth to booth. It's a great way to sample a lot of wines without the pressure to buy you may feel when you visit the wineries.

Where the wines are
APPELLATIONS CONTRÔLÉES

1. Côtes-du-Rhône Villages
2. Gigondas
3. Vacqueyras
4. Beaumes-de-Venise
5. Châteauneuf-du-Pape
6. Côtes du Ventoux
7. Côtes du Luberon
8. Coteaux de Pierrevert
9. Coteaux d'Aix-en-Provence
10. Les Baux de Provence
11. Palette

12. Coteaux Varois
13. Côtes de Provence
14. Cassis
15. Bandol

Lirac
Tavel
Avignon
Arles
RHÔNE
Lourmarin
Aix
Marseille
Cassis
Bandol
MEDITERRANEAN

Dégustation

You can buy local wines at the supermarket but it's more fun to visit the wineries and taste. Look for a sign like dégustation de vin or cave ouvert. In some areas like Tavel and Gigondas we've taken advantage of a maison de vin, a center which showcases the wines of many local producers.

Calling ahead for an appointment may be necessary at some châteaux (Trevallon, e.g.), but most welcome walk-ins and have tasting rooms. Like everything else in Provence, many shut down for several hours around lunchtime.

Most wineries are friendly and eager to show off their wines. Once we tracked down a white wine we had enjoyed at a restaurant, but the proprietor "refused" to sell it to us until we had tasted his red wine. It was even better.

Inside the tasting room there will be several wines to taste, along with a price list so you'll know what you're getting into. You may want to taste a white, rosé and red, or perhaps a range of reds of different years and prices. The server will offer them in the proper order, saving the best for last. The tastings are free (unless otherwise noted) but we usually buy at least one bottle.

Except at larger, more tourist-friendly wineries, few employees speak English. This may reduce the benefit of any technical information they may impart, but the important thing is how the wine tastes. Which brings us to the troubling question: to swallow or not to swallow?

The ritual goes like this: look at the wine in the glass to judge its color. Swirl it and sniff, to savor the aroma or "nose." Then swish it in your mouth and spit it out. If you insist on swallowing, as we inevitably do, pace yourself. Repeated tastings can impair motor skills.

Château de Mayol **

Château de Mille **

APT

Château de l'Isolette **

Château la Canorgue **

BONNIEUX

A tasting tour of the Côtes du Luberon
SWALLOWERS: DO NOT ATTEMPT IN ONE DAY

**** Château la Verrerie

*** Château Constantin Chevalier

Château La Sable *

LOURMARIN

CUCURON

Cellier du Marrenan **

LAURIS

Domaine de la Cavale *

** Château Turcan

ANSOUIS

LA TOUR d'AIGUES

CADENET

Château Saint Pierre de Mejans ***

Château Val Joanis ***

(* Personal Rating)

PERTUIS

The king who wouldn't spit

Long ago, in sunny Provence, there lived a king who loved to drink wine. He loved a fruity rosé with his lunch and he loved a regal red with dinner. Between meals the king liked to visit the wineries of the region and sample their wares. His Royal Taster would take a mouthful of each wine, swish it around, then spit it out. If he declared the wine fit for a king, the king would take a long drink. All afternoon the taster would sip, swish and spit and the king would drink. "You know, Sire," said the taster, "you can taste the wine without swallowing it." "Spit out good wine?" said the king. "What a waste!" With that the king took another long swig, smiled, and passed out.

moral:

It is better if the wine is the one who gets wasted.

A Moveable Feast

Each year, to promote their wines, Rasteau holds the *Escapade des Gourmets*, a 5-course, 5k walk through the vineyards. For $25* you take your wine glass from station to station. Stop One: *mise-en-bouche* (a small plate with olives, olive bread, *pissaladière* (onion-anchovy tart) and spinach quiche served with Rasteau blanc. At some stops there was musical entertainment. We finished three hours later with cake, a glass of Rasteau's famous *vin doux naturel* and coffee. A truly unique experience!

*2002

Other wines and sights near Rasteau

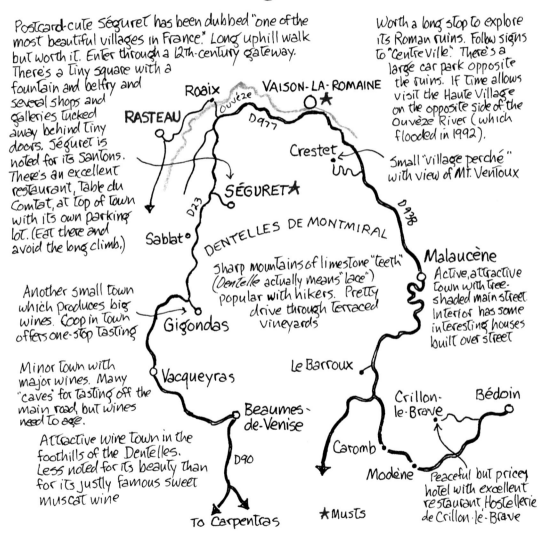

Postcard-cute Séguret has been dubbed "one of the most beautiful villages in France." Long uphill walk but worth it. Enter through a 12th-century gateway. There's a tiny square with a fountain and belfry and several shops and galleries tucked away behind tiny doors. Séguret is noted for its Santons. There's an excellent restaurant, Table du Comtat, at top of town with its own parking lot. (Eat there and avoid the long climb.)

Worth a long stop to explore its Roman ruins. Follow signs to "Centre Ville." There's a large car park opposite the ruins. If time allows visit the Haute Village on the opposite side of the Ouvèze River (which flooded in 1992).

Small "village perché" with view of Mt. Ventoux

Another small town which produces big wines. Coop in town offers one-stop tasting

Minor town with major wines. Many "caves" for tasting off the main road, but wines need to age.

Attractive wine town in the foothills of the Dentelles. Less noted for its beauty than for its justly famous sweet muscat wine

Active, attractive town with tree-shaded main street. Interior has some interesting houses built over street

Peaceful but pricey hotel with excellent restaurant, Hostellerie de Crillon-le-Brave

Map labels

Roaix
Ouvèze
VAISON-LA-ROMAINE ★
RASTEAU
D977
Crestet
SÉGURET ★
D23
DENTELLES DE MONTMIRAL
Sablat
Malaucène
D938

Sharp mountains of limestone "teeth" (Dentelle actually means "lace") popular with hikers. Pretty drive through terraced vineyards

Gigondas
Vacqueyras
Le Barroux
Crillon-le-Brave
Bédoin
Beaumes-de-Venise
Caromb
Modène
D90
To Carpentras
★ Musts

The Little Car that couldn't

There once was a little car who hated to drive in France because the other cars frightened him. They would speed up behind him, blink their lights, then speed past. They rode his rear bumper and generally made life on the road worrisome. ∞ Then one day, mysteriously, they were all gone. The little car was the only car on the road. ∞ He drove along narrow country roads and never saw another car. He drove into the centers of towns and never saw another car. Now he loved to drive in France. ∞ Relaxed and happy after a day of carefree driving, the little car was headed home along a narrow mountain road. Suddenly, from out of nowhere, a speeding Citroën loomed in his rear-view mirror, rode his bumper, and nearly forced the little car off the shoulderless road.

moral:

If there is only one other car in France it will be behind you, trying to pass.

Driving in Provence

First, the good news: driving is a great way to see Provence. You are free to go wherever you want. There are highspeed autoroutes to cover distances expediently and scenic "green roads" (so designated on the essential detailed Michelin maps) for leisurely meandering in the country.

Now the bad news: you are not alone. And everyone else on the road is in a big hurry. As your rearview mirror warns: objects are closer than they appear. Actually, driving in Provence is no worse than driving anywhere where the roads are narrow, unpatrolled and where it is a matter of national pride to never be behind another motorist on the highway. You could easily spend all your driving time in a state of road rage, but just remember that the driver riding your rear bumper is not out to annoy you personally, he's just hurrying home for lunch.

There are three categories of roads: Autoroutes, "N" roads and "D" roads.

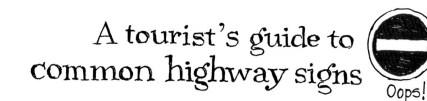

A tourist's guide to common highway signs

Oops!

| Dead End
Try again | O.K.
One way
your way | Try again
One way
their way | O.K., barely
They have
right-of-way | Road ahead
gets even
narrower | YIELD.
Always a
good idea | Nothing
good
ahead! |

Autoroutes are essentially proving grounds for Mercedes class cars whose goal is to get you from one city to another in less time than the T.G.V. And you have to pay to play. They are toll (péage) roads. When you approach a toll plaza look for a lane marked with a "man" sign, especially if you don't know the toll or don't have correct change.

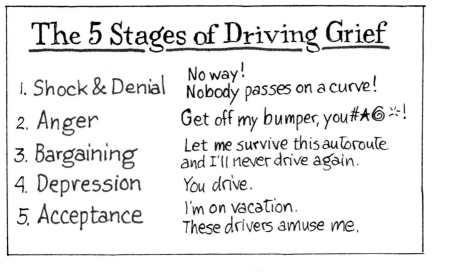

The 5 Stages of Driving Grief

1. Shock & Denial   No way! Nobody passes on a curve!

2. Anger   Get off my bumper, you #★◎☼!

3. Bargaining   Let me survive this autoroute and I'll never drive again.

4. Depression   You drive.

5. Acceptance   I'm on vacation. These drivers amuse me.

110 — Suggested minimum speed

NO — Resume excessive speed

NO PARKING (optional)

Watch your left!

Watch your head!

CENTRE VILLE — Proceed at your own risk

"N" roads (routes nationales) are similar to a basic U.S. highway: well-groomed and wide enough to have a white line down the center. Watch out for those with a third lane in the middle, a passing lane for whoever gets there first.

"D" roads vary greatly. They are two-lane, but on some you're not completely sure. Alongside, if there is not a sheer cliff, there may be a deep drainage ditch. Faced with an oncoming car straddling the middle of the road, a driver faces two unpleasant options-- a head-on collision or veering into the ditch. Luckily there is a third choice: hug the side and pray that the oncoming car will share the road. Somehow they always do.

Probably the only car in Provence you will be able to pass.

Driving in Provence is, ideally, a two-person job requiring a driver with steely nerves, patience and quick reflexes and a navigator with good eyes, a calm manner and a detailed (Michelin) map.

At any given moment the navigator should know the name of the <u>major town</u> you're headed for and the name of the <u>next small town</u> you'll pass through on the route you want to take. (There are often several ways to get to your destination, some more direct than others.) Town names are often more useful than route numbers, which seem to change on a whim and may fail to identify themselves until after you've committed to a turn. It's town names you look for in that cluster of directional signs you'll encounter.

The roundabout is the tourist's savior. As you enter a traffic circle (remembering to yield to traffic on your left – vous n'avez pas la priorité) your options will be posted. "Out at 9 o'clock!" shouts the navigator, so you drive three-quarters of the way around and exit. Don't panic. If you're unsure of the exit simply go around again while the navigator double-checks the map. Inside a roundabout is one of the fews times you will have the right-of-way (priorité).

Rest areas (aires) are frequent on autoroutes. They may be parking areas only or full service (gasoline, food, restrooms). You pump your own gasoline and go inside to pay. The posted price for fuel seems reasonable until you remember it is per __liter__, not per gallon. Figure on about $70 to fill your tank.

A few useful words			
		deviation	detour
essence	gasoline	sauf riverains	except for residents
gazole	diesel	route barree	no thoroughfare
sans plomb	unleaded	cedez le passage	yield right-of-way
peage	toll	à droite	right
stationnement interdit	no parking	à gauche	left
sens unique	one-way	le pneu	tire

The Outfoxed Fox

Once there was a fox who loved to go to market. Because he lived too far away to walk to town, the fox bought a car. But when he drove to town on market day he couldn't find a parking place nearby. In fact, by the time he found a place he was almost back home. So the fox hatched a sly plan. He sneaked into town, found a prime spot and put up a handicapped parking sign next to it. Then he put a handicapped parking sticker on his car. "Now," thought the sly fox, "I'll be assured a place to park." On market day he confidently drove to town. But when he got to his "handicapped" parking place, not only was a car parked there but another car was double parked behind it.

moral:

People who park on sidewalks are not likely to be fooled by handicapped parking signs.

Parking

There are two basic schools of thought when it comes to parking: (1) drive as close as possible and hope someone will be pulling out of a place, or (2) grab the first available place within reasonable walking distance. The passenger tends to favor the first, the driver usually prefers the second.

The Driver's Friend

Stationnement Payant

If your street or lot is designated payant you have to pay. There may be someone collecting as you enter. More likely there will be a machine (horodateur) where you must get a ticket to display on your dashboard.

In bigger city underground lots you will get a ticket which you keep with you. When you return, take it to the caisse before you go to your car, pay, and use the validated ticket to get out the automated gate. Be sure to remember where your car is. We once took so long to find ours that by the time we reached the gate our validated ticket was no longer valid.

MARKET

In your dreams!

This is your best parking opportunity

The Full Sidewalk
Damn the pedestrians, full speed ahead, up & on.

The Half-Sidewalk Straddle
Compromise in which both pedestrians and other drivers have half a chance of getting past.

The Simple Double
Parallel to a presumed longer term parker. May leave lights blinking to signal intent to return.

The 2-for-1 Double
Parallel to two pull-in parkers, sealing off both cars.
Double the pleasure, double the fun

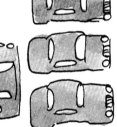

The Temporarily Handicapped
How often do disabled drivers really need those prime location spots anyway?

l'Abandonnment!
A personal favorite. Driver pulled up onto traffic control island in middle of busiest intersection in town on market day. Note blinking lights for nice added sense of emergency.

A GUIDE TO BASIC PARKING TECHNIQUES

The typical American tourist tends to look for a "parking place," i.e, a gap along the curb between two parked cars large enough to hold his car with space front and rear. The French simply drive to where they want to go and park there.

The fox & the crow

Once there was a crow with a natural ability to get around. He could soar high above the trees and read the landscape like a map. He always flew by the most direct route and never got lost. ⟳ One day he visited Aix-en-Provence. As he was sitting at a cafe sipping a cup of coffee he spotted a fox walking up the Cours toward him. The fox looked hungry so the crow took off. Sure enough, the hungry fox took off after him. As always, the crow flew straight out of town. But the fox soon became lost in the maze of one-way streets, alleys and pedestrian walks.

moral:

You can't always get out of town as the crow flies.

AIX-en-PROVENCE
Once you've parked, you'll love it.

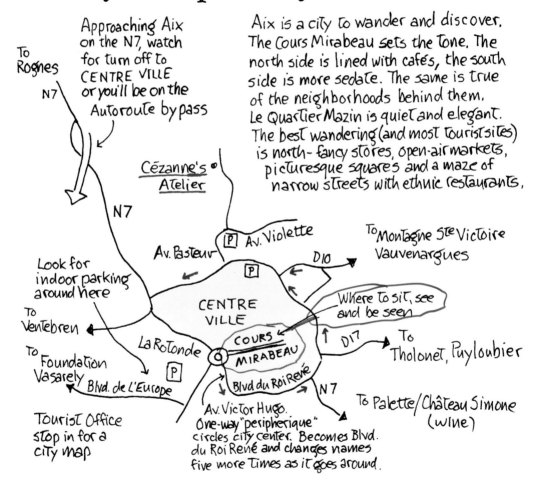

Approaching Aix on the N7, watch for turn off to CENTRE VILLE or you'll be on the Autoroute bypass

Aix is a city to wander and discover. The Cours Mirabeau sets the tone. The north side is lined with cafés, the south side is more sedate. The same is true of the neighborhoods behind them. Le Quartier Mazin is quiet and elegant. The best wandering (and most tourist sites) is north- fancy stores, open-air markets, picturesque squares and a maze of narrow streets with ethnic restaurants.

To Rognes

N7

N7

Cézanne's Atelier

P Av. Violette

Av. Pasteur

D10

To Montagne Ste Victoire Vauvenargues

P

CENTRE VILLE

Where to sit, see and be seen

Look for indoor parking around here

To Ventebren

La Rotonde

COURS MIRABEAU

D17

To Tholonet, Puyloubier

To Foundation Vasarely

P

Blvd. de L'Europe

Blvd du Roi René

N7

To Palette/Château Simone (wine)

Tourist Office stop in for a city map

Av. Victor Hugo. One-way "peripherique" circles city center. Becomes Blvd. du Roi René and changes names five more times as it goes around.

ATELIER CÉZANNE

Leave the Old Quarter past St. Saveur Cathedral, walk up Av. Pasteur, and climb up Av. Paul Cézanne to visit Cézanne's studio and garden

uphill climb

Av. Paul Cézanne

Av. de la Violette

Clos de Violette
Good, but expensive restaurant

Av. Pasteur

Blvd Aristide Briand

OLD QUARTER

Outdoor flower markets, café-lined squares, narrow, winding streets, aromatic ethnic restaurants combine to make Aix a wanderer's paradise.

You could, and perhaps should, visit the museums, churches and historic buildings scattered throughout the city. Or you could rest your feet and experience the charm of Aix from a café table on the Cours Mirabeau. With the possible exception of Deux Magots in Paris, no cafés in France offer a better show.

The mile-long Cours was built in 1649 and the first café opened in the mid-18th century. It is still the place to see and be seen. For the price of a cup of coffee (not the cheapest cup you'll ever have) you can settle back and observe the art of the 3-cheek kiss as café habitués greet one another. Les Deux Garçons is the most famous of the Cours cafés. Another good choice is Le Grillon. If you use their tiny restroom you'll discover a charming upstairs dining room.) These are all café-restaurants, which means they serve full meals at lunchtime. (Don't sit at a tablecloth if all you want is a drink.)

Besides the Cours, you might try a table on Place de Verdon on market day or Place de l'Hôtel de Ville where the flower market is held.

Les Deux Garcons

Comin' 'round the Montagne Ste Victoire

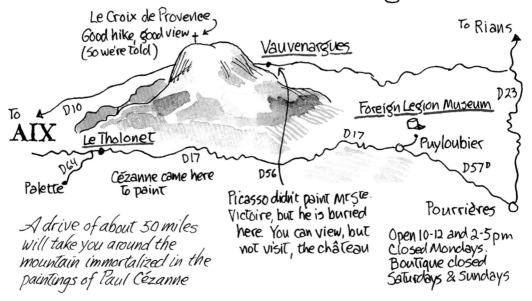

Le Croix de Provence, Good hike, good view (so we're told)

To Rians

Vauvenargues

Foreign Legion Museum

D23

To **AIX**

D10

Le Tholonet

D17

Puyloubier

D64

D17

D56

D57ᴰ

Palette

Cézanne came here to paint

Picasso didn't paint Mt Ste. Victoire, but he is buried here. You can view, but not visit, the château

Pourrières

A drive of about 50 miles will take you around the mountain immortalized in the paintings of Paul Cézanne

Open 10-12 and 2-5pm Closed Mondays. Boutique closed Saturdays & Sundays

For an offbeat wine, may we suggest a modest "Foreign Legion Red." Just west of Puyloubier you'll find the "Institution des Invalides de la Legion Etrangère." The hospital is home to the "must-see" Foreign Legion Museum. You can tour three rooms of uniforms and equipment of the Legion throughout its history. (Some aging mannequins are missing hands, an unintentional reminder of the horrors of war.) The museum is but a prelude to the Boutique. The distinctive legionnaire hat (kèpi) is interpreted in a variety of ceramic creations including the popular crèche scene in upturned kèpi. The Côtes de Provence wine they sell under their own Legion Etrangère label (red, white and rosé) is reasonably priced and is a reasonably good picnic companion.

Château de Vauvenargues

Blue water, white wine

DOMAINE DU PATERNEL
Blanc de Blancs
Cassis
appellation Cassis contrôlée

L B1

Produit de France

37,5cl

mis en bouteille par
E.A.R.L. SANTINI
Propriétaire-Récoltant
Domaine du Paternel
13260 CASSIS
FRANCE

12% vol

MIS EN BOUTEILLE AU DOMAINE

The pleasures of CASSIS ("cah-see")

Less chic than St Tropez, less industrial than La Ciotat, this little fishing port actually has some working fishing boats among the yachts and tour boats in its picturesque harbor. Tour boats visit *les Calanques*,* remote inlets surrounded by steep white cliffs. The secluded nature of these coves makes them popular with nude sunbathers, though fans of the topless need only stroll the in-town beach. There's a small park, folk museum and casino, but mostly Cassis is a place to enjoy fresh seafood and the local *blanc de blanc*.

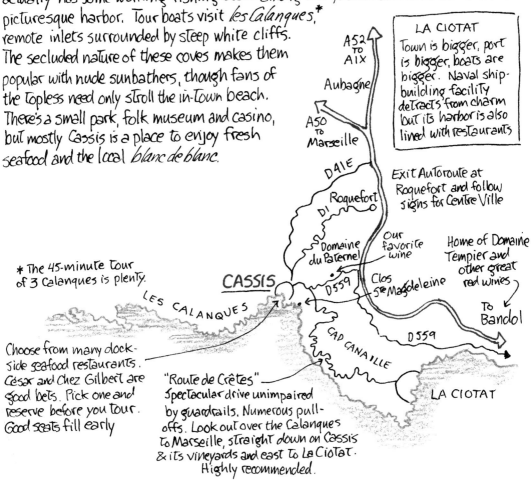

LA CIOTAT
Town is bigger, port is bigger, boats are bigger. Naval ship-building facility detracts from charm but its harbor is also lined with restaurants

A52 TO AIX

Aubagne

A50 TO Marseille

D41E

Roquefort

Exit Autoroute at Roquefort and follow signs for Centre Ville

D1

Domaine du Paternel

Our favorite wine

Home of Domaine Tempier and other great red wines

* The 45-minute tour of 3 Calanques is plenty.

CASSIS

D559

Clos Ste Magdeleine

To Bandol

LES CALANQUES

CAP CANAILLE

D559

LA CIOTAT

Choose from many dock-side seafood restaurants. César and Chez Gilbert are good bets. Pick one and reserve before you tour. Good seats fill early

"Route de Crêtes" Spectacular drive unimpaired by guardrails. Numerous pull-offs. Look out over the Calanques to Marseille, straight down on Cassis & its vineyards and east to La Ciotat. Highly recommended.

A search for Santons

These ubiquitous clay figurines in traditional Provençal costumes are certainly not difficult to find. A famous *santonnier* lived next door to the house we rented and there are santons in almost every souvenir shop in Provence. Their quality varies, but we've found some we especially like. They are not the big Barbie Doll-size figures in stiff cloth outfits. They are little hand-painted clay figures made by a couple, Hélène and Guy Troussier, in the tiny remote village of Vernèques. Vernèques is something of an artist colony, with studios of a potter, sculptor, woodworker, painter and "faïencier d'Art." (Six artisans may not seem like much of a colony, but as a percentage

of the total population it's significant.) The Toussiers have a tiny shop. If no one is there, ring the bell and Hélène will scurry over from their house next door.

If santon shopping makes you thirsty, stop at Château Bas, a winery constructed on the site of a Gallo-Roman village. Check in at the tasting room and they will direct you along a tree-shaded path to the rear of the château and there, indeed, are the remains (two columns) of a 1ST century Roman temple.

And the wines are excellent.

Village off the main road with a sad history of religious persecution. Memorial to the massacre of the Waldenses in 1545.

Merindol

D973

To LOURMARIN

Lauris

LA DURANCE

To senas
CAYAILLON

Mallemort

Cadenet

Good view of
Alleins and its
chateau as
you approach
(or depart)

Alleins

Pont Royal

Charleval

D561

la Roque
d'Anthéron

Silvacane

Vieux
Vernèques
(ruins)

D22

More wine?
Watch closely for
Chateau Pont Royal.
It's right on the road

Cistercian Abbey
(like Sénanque,
near Gordes)
Built between
1175 and 1300.
Worth a visit.

D220

Cazan

Vernèques

D220

D22

The ruins of "old
Vernèques" are closed
to the public but there
are good views from
the grounds

Chateau
Bas ★★★

To
la Barben

Try their rosé
(Pierres du sud)
or their Cuvée du
Temple rouge

To Lambesc
Aix-en-Provence

Les Alpilles

Les Alpilles (little Alps) are, geologically, an extension of the Luberons, but quite different in appearance. The Luberons are green and tree-covered. The Alpilles are stark, bleached gray, with much exposed rock.

A favorite drive begins in Maussane and ends, in the best of times, with lunch at Bistrot d'Eygalières ("Chez Bru"). More often we settle for a picnic somewhere along the way. Take the D78 to tiny le Destet, then left on the D24. Perhaps the wildest stretch of scenery is the D25 east to the lonely castle ruin, Castelas de Roquemartin. The D69 north is wider, the terrain more open. At Orgon, take the D24B to Eygalières. Numerous signs indicate that Resistance hero Jean Moulin was active around here, but the Gestapo had more luck following his "route" than we have had. Eygalières makes a nice stop, even without lunch at the Bistrot.

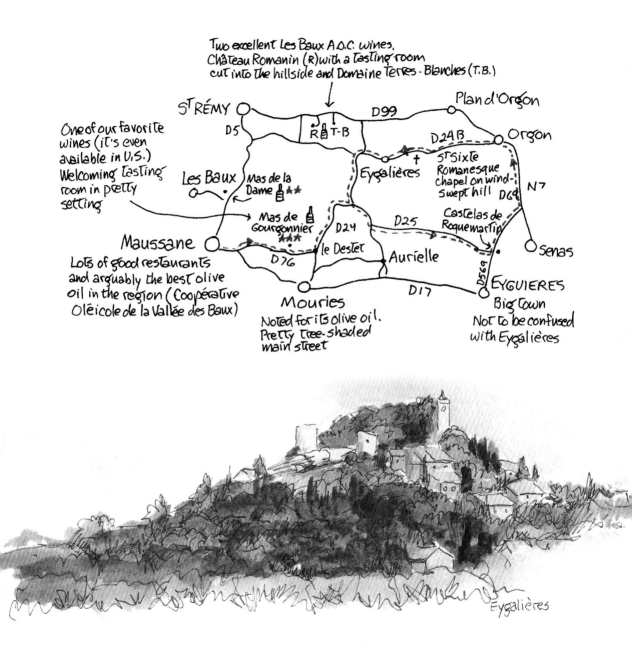

Two excellent Les Baux A.O.C. wines.
Château Romanin (R) with a tasting room
cut into the hillside and Domaine Terres-Blanches (T.B.)

Plan d'Orgon

ST RÉMY

D99

D5

R T-B

One of our favorite
wines (it's even
available in U.S.)
Welcoming tasting
room in pretty
setting

D24B

Orgon

Eygalières

St Sixte
Romanesque
chapel on wind-
swept hill

N7

D69

Les Baux

Mas de la
Dame ★★

Mas de
Gourgonnier
★★★

D24

D25

Castelas de
Roquemartin

le Dester

Senas

Maussane

Aurielle

D76

D569

EYGUIERES

Lots of good restaurants
and arguably the best olive
oil in the region (Coopérative
Oléicole de la Vallée des Baux)

Mouries

D17

Big town
Not to be confused
with Eygalières

Noted for its olive oil.
Pretty tree-shaded
main street

Eygalières

Les Baux

Over 1.5 million people visit this classic site each year (second only to Mont St Michel) so you'd be well advised to get there early, before the tour buses descend, or more correctly, ascend, for this feudal fortress is perched high on a rocky crag of the Alpilles. The castle and ramparts were destroyed in 1633 at the urging of Cardinal Richelieu. The eerie remains were evocative even before the addition of some reconstructed catapults and siege machines. The ruins of old Les Baux ("Ville Morte") and the spectacular views of the vineyards and olive groves below are reached by going through the "new" village. You must run a gauntlet of souvenir shops, crêperies and galleries. There are some small museums, including one of santons, but you'll want to hurry to the top.

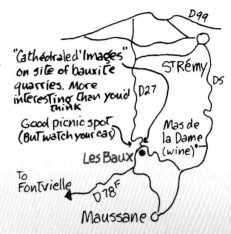

"Cathédrale d'Images" on site of bauxite quarries. More interesting than you'd think

Good picnic spot (But watch your car)

St Rémy

D27

D5

D99

Mas de la Dame (wine)

Les Baux

To Fontvieille

D 78F

Maussane

FINDS NEAR FONTVIEILLE

An ancient aqueduct, a fine wine and a popular restaurant

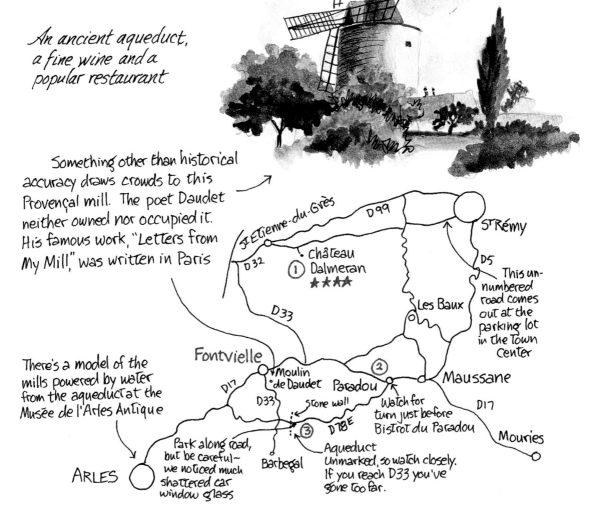

Something other than historical accuracy draws crowds to this Provençal mill. The poet Daudet neither owned nor occupied it. His famous work, "Letters from My Mill," was written in Paris

There's a model of the mills powered by water from the aqueduct at the Musée de l'Arles Antique

St Etienne-du-Grès

D99

St Rémy

D32

① Château Dalmeran
★★★

D5

This un-numbered road comes out at the parking lot in the town center

D33

Les Baux

Fontvieille

▾Moulin de Daudet

② Paradou

Maussane

D17

D33

Stone wall

Watch for turn just before Bistrot du Paradou

D17

Mouries

Park along road, but be careful— we noticed much shattered car window glass

Barbegal

③ D78E

Aqueduct unmarked, so watch closely. If you reach D33 you've gone too far.

ARLES

① CHÂTEAU DALMERAN

We first tasted Château Dalmeran at Le Bistrot d'Eygalières in 2001. The winery is on a one-lane country road between St Rémy and St Etiennes-du-Grès. It was recently purchased by an extremely hospitable Brit who is restoring the château. We showed up to buy some wine in 2007 and were treated to a 2-hour tour and tasting, plus a free bottle of rosé. We can't guarantee you free wine, but it is excellent, especially the red.

② Bistrot du Paradou

This is one of our favorite places to eat. Very friendly, very local. Tile floor, marble-topped iron tables and a bar that runs the length of the room. It offers a set prix fixe menu (check the board outside) which includes entrée, plat, fromage and dessert, plus wine (a bottle of house *vin rouge* is on the table) and coffee.

③ L'Aqueduc de Barbegal

Walk south alongside an olive grove past arches and fragments until you reach a gap in the rocks. Step through and look down the hill. It is here that the Romans built 16 waterwheels powered by the aqueduct

St RÉMY

St Rémy's size and location make it an ideal home base from which to tour the Alpilles. Les Baux is just minutes away. St Rémy has impressive Roman treasures. "Les Antiques" - an Arc de Triomphe and an unusual funerary monument, the Mausolée des Jules -- are so easily seen from the road that it's tempting not to stop for a closer look. Glanum, a Roman town still being excavated, ranks with major classical sites in Provence. Vincent Van Gogh was hospitalized at the nearby St Paul de Mausole and you can see several of his painting locations. The town has lots of good restaurants and a marvelous Wednesday market (which complicates parking).

St Paul-de-Mausole

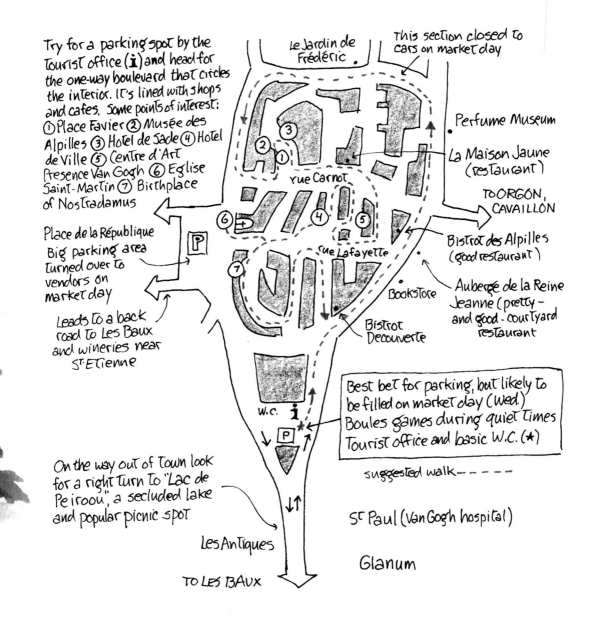

Try for a parking spot by the Tourist office (ℹ) and head for the one-way boulevard that circles the interior. It's lined with shops and cafes. Some points of interest: ① Place Favier ② Musée des Alpilles ③ Hôtel de Sade ④ Hôtel de Ville ⑤ Centre d'Art Presence Van Gogh ⑥ Eglise Saint-Martin ⑦ Birthplace of Nostradamus

Le Jardin de Frédéric

This section closed to cars on market day

Perfume Museum

La Maison Jaune (restaurant)

TOORGON, CAVAILLON

rue Carnot

Bistrot des Alpilles (good restaurant)

Auberge de la Reine Jeanne (pretty - and good - courtyard restaurant

rue Lafayette

Bookstore

Bistrot Decouverte

Place de la République
Big parking area turned over to vendors on market day

Leads to a back road to Les Baux and wineries near St Etienne

W.C.

Best bet for parking, but likely to be filled on market day (Wed.) Boules games during quiet times Tourist office and basic W.C. (*)

suggested walk ------

On the way out of town look for a right turn to "Lac de Peiroou", a secluded lake and popular picnic spot

St Paul (Van Gogh hospital)

Les Antiques

Glanum

TO LES BAUX

Sights around St Rémy

Maillane is noted for being the birthplace of Frederic Mistral. At Graveson there is a much advertised perfume museum. Take the drive to Barbentane via St Michel de Frigolet. The latter is an abbey in a restful forested setting. The monks make a liqueur of note. Barbentane has a grand château you can visit. Boulbon is in the ruins category. You need only a short stop to see the interesting Chapel of St Gabriel.

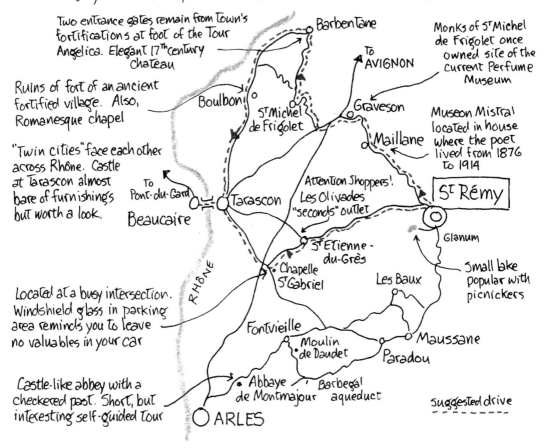

Two entrance gates remain from town's fortifications at foot of the Tour Angelica. Elegant 17th century chateau

Ruins of fort of an ancient fortified village. Also, Romanesque chapel

"Twin cities" face each other across Rhône. Castle at Tarascon almost bare of furnishings but worth a look.

Located at a busy intersection. Windshield glass in parking area reminds you to leave no valuables in your car

Castle-like abbey with a checkered past. Short, but interesting self-guided tour

Monks of St Michel de Frigolet once owned site of the current Perfume Museum

Museon Mistral located in house where the poet lived from 1876 to 1914

Attention Shoppers! Les Olivades "seconds" outlet

Small lake popular with picnickers

Barbentane

To AVIGNON

Boulbon

St Michel de Frigolet

Graveson

Maillane

St Rémy

Glanum

To Pont-du-Gard

Tarascon

Beaucaire

St Etienne-du-Grès

Chapelle St Gabriel

Les Baux

RHÔNE

Fontvieille

Moulin de Daudet

Maussane

Paradou

Abbaye de Montmajour

Barbegal aqueduct

suggested drive

ARLES

View of Beaucaire

Beaucaire was the site of one of the largest fairs in medieval Europe, launched in 1217. Its chateau overlooks the Town, which has a little "waterfront" of shops and cafes along a canal.

Tarascon's chateau sits right at the river's edge and was home to the court of Good King René in the 15th century. The Town is also famous for Tarasque, a part lion, part crocodile monster, the character Tartarin created by Alphonse Daudet and for the Musée Souleiado (provençal fabrics).

Château at Tarascon

A walk around ARLES

Pick up a map at the tourist office (i) across from the Jardin d'Été, one of the few green areas in this tightly packed town. Walk up to Place de la République with its ancient obelisk, fountain and loitering youth. Across from the Hotel de Ville is the Romanesque Eglise St Trophime, much admired for its carved portal. Be sure to visit the calming courtyard of the Cloisters. Walk up Rue de la Calade to the first of the Roman remains, the Théâtre Antique. The theater is still used, so the tiers of plastic chairs detract from the sense of history. Just beyond the theater is the Roman Amphithéâtre, still used for bullfights. Head down Rue Voltaire to the bustling Place Voltaire, then browse your way to the Eglise St Julien, past some antique shops to Musée Réattu (paintings and drawings). On the opposite corner are the Thermes de Constantin, ruins of Roman baths which require some imagination to visualize.

Then wend your way up Rue du Savage to the social hub of Arles, Place du Forum. Two columns to the left of Hotel Nord-Pinus are all that remain of its ancient past. (The square is not actually on the site of a Roman forum. Neither is Café de la Nuit just as Van Gogh painted it. Its gaudy yellow façade tries to recreate the effect of his nighttime scene.) Check out the interior decor of Hotel Nord-Pinus, especially the funky little bar. The statue looming over the café umbrellas in the Place is Frédéric Mistral, whose Museon Arlaten is just around the corner. The poet used his Nobel Prize money to preserve, it would seem, every artifact of Provençal life. The underground galleries of the Cryptoportico are another Roman sight worth seeing. Finally, turn down to the Espace Van Gogh, the former hospital where Vincent was a patient. The area nearby is loaded with stores, so you can shop your way back or stop at McDonald's for a Big Mac.

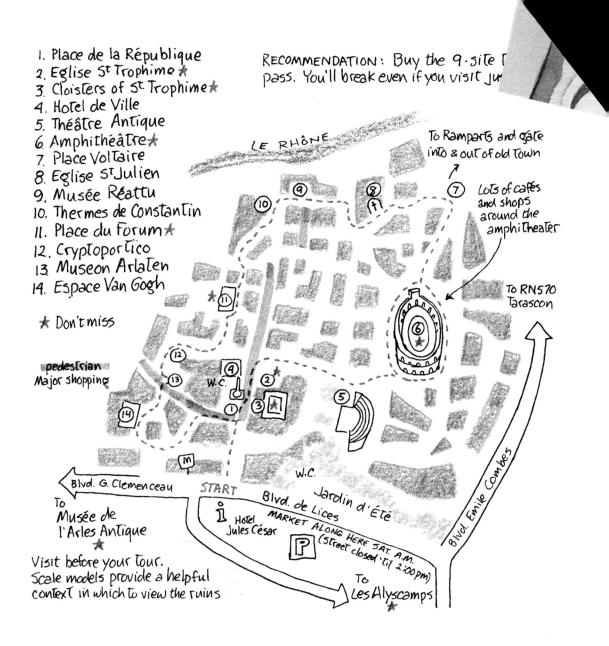

1. Place de la République
2. Eglise St Trophime ★
3. Cloisters of St Trophime ★
4. Hotel de Ville
5. Théâtre Antique
6. Amphithéâtre ★
7. Place Voltaire
8. Eglise St Julien
9. Musée Réattu
10. Thermes de Constantin
11. Place du Forum ★
12. Cryptoportico
13. Museon Arlaten
14. Espace Van Gogh

★ Don't miss

pedestrian
Major shopping

RECOMMENDATION: Buy the 9-site [...]
pass. You'll break even if you visit ju[...]

LE RHÔNE

To Ramparts and gate
into & out of old Town

Lots of cafés
and shops
around the
amphitheater

To RN570
Tarascon

Blvd. G. Clemenceau

To
Musée de
l'Arles Antique
★
Visit before your tour.
Scale models provide a helpful
context in which to view the ruins

START

Blvd. de Lices

Hotel
Jules César

MARKET ALONG HERE SAT. A.M.

(street closed 'til 2:00pm)

Jardin d'Été

W.C.

Blvd. Emile Combes

To
Les Alyscamps
★

A bridge not too far (and not to be missed!)

There are many routes to the impressive Roman aqueduct, Pont-du-Gard. Plan to take one of them. Despite "improvements" it should be on everyone's must-see list of ancient sites in Provence.

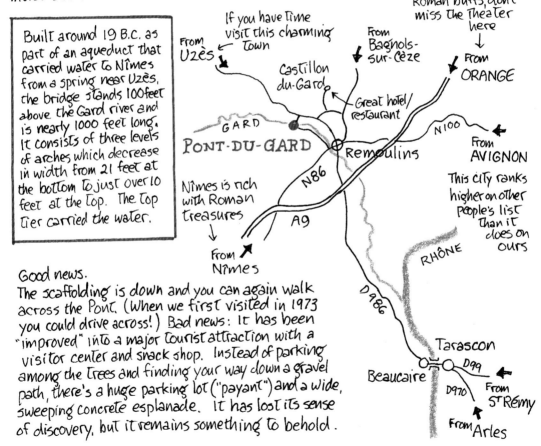

Built around 19 B.C. as part of an aqueduct that carried water to Nîmes from a spring near Uzès, the bridge stands 100 feet above the Gard river and is nearly 1000 feet long. It consists of three levels of arches which decrease in width from 21 feet at the bottom to just over 10 feet at the top. The top tier carried the water.

If you have time visit this charming town

From Uzès

Roman buffs, don't miss the Theater here ↓ From ORANGE

From Bagnols-sur-Cèze

Castillon du-Gard

Great hotel/restaurant

GARD

PONT-DU-GARD ⊕ Remoulins

N100

From AVIGNON

N86

This city ranks higher on other people's list than it does on ours

Nîmes is rich with Roman treasures ↓

A9

RHÔNE

From Nîmes

D986

Tarascon

D99

Beaucaire

D970   From ST REMY

From Arles

Good news.
The scaffolding is down and you can again walk across the Pont. (When we first visited in 1973 you could drive across!) Bad news: It has been "improved" into a major tourist attraction with a visitor center and snack shop. Instead of parking among the trees and finding your way down a gravel path, there's a huge parking lot ("payant") and a wide, sweeping concrete esplanade. It has lost its sense of discovery, but it remains something to behold.

The woman who lived in the toilette

Once upon a time there was a woman who lived in a toilette. Really. It was an underground public toilet in the heart of Aix-en-Provence. She had it fixed up as prettily as she could with religious figurines and assorted *objets de brocante*. She had even set up a cute teddy bear tea party. She sat down there in her cozy toilet home watching TV and collecting money from everyone who came down to use the facilities. She provided no apparent service except to provide the facilities.

There was no tea in the teddy bears' teacups.

moral:

A public toilet is a nice place to visit but you wouldn't want to live there.

W.C.s

No amount of pre-planning can prevent the occasional need to go while you're out and about. Here are some tips:

① Always avail yourself of a "toilet of opportunity." You never know when the next one will come along.

② Use cafés. Buy a coffee and become a "customer."

③ Forget about privacy. In France, privacy means facing away from traffic when going alongside the highway.

④ Carry your own paper.

A FIVE STAR RATING SYSTEM FOR PUBLIC W.C.s

★★★★★ Just like home. Clean, private stalls with seats on toilets that flush. Paper. Hot and cold running water. Towels. Lights. (Rare)

★★★★ Clean, well-stocked and pre-lighted

★★★ Sorta clean. You can sit but may or may not have paper. May have to grope for light switch. Lights may be on short timer.

★★ Bowl with seat removed. Hunkering only. If no light, you may be thankful.

★ Footprints and hole. Takes practice. Stand well back before pulling flush chain.

(No stars) Same as above, but no flush.

PROPOSED INTERNATIONAL SIGNAGE FOR PUBLIC W.C.s

Plastic Seat

Seatless Bowl

Footprints

Payment Expected

Even in Provence, every day can't be sunny.